Charge delivered to the clergy and churchwardens of the Diocese of Lincoln : at his primary visitation, October, 1886

Church of England. Diocese of Lincoln. Bishop (1885-1910 : King)

Au 185?

CHARGE

DELIVERED TO

THE CLERGY AND CHURCHWARDENS

OF THE

DIOCESE OF LINCOLN,

AT HIS

PRIMARY VISITATION,

OCTOBER, 1886,

BY

EDWARD,
LORD BISHOP OF LINCOLN.

Lincoln: JAMES WILLIAMSON, 290, HIGH STREET.
Oxford & London: PARKER & CO.

TO THE

CLERGY AND CHURCHWARDENS

OF THE

DIOCESE OF LINCOLN,

This Charge

IS AFFECTIONATELY AND RESPECTFULLY

DEDICATED,

BY THEIR FAITHFUL FRIEND AND SERVANT,

E. LINCOLN.

HILTON HOUSE, LINCOLN,
F. of St. Hugh, 1886.

ANALYSIS OF CHARGE.

ANALYSIS OF CHARGE.

My Rev. Brethren, and my Brethren of the Laity,

ACCORDING to the usual custom of this Diocese, the Bishop's Visitation should have been held last year, that is, after an interval of three years : but, as not more than half that period of time has elapsed since it pleased God to entrust me with the spiritual oversight of this great Diocese, I was advised by some persons to postpone this my Primary Visitation for another year and a half, until I should be better acquainted with my own duties and your needs.

The advantages of such postponement are obvious, and yet I have thought it better, on the whole, to issue the questions of inquiry, and to hold this Visitation, that at least you might be assured of my readiness to do my best to serve you, trusting to your forbearance and kindness if the object of this Visitation is as much for my own instruction as yours, so that we may learn together to serve our God more acceptably in the years that may remain.

Short as the time is, during which I have been amongst you, my brethren, it has been long enough to afford us good reasons for serious reflexion ; no less than 23 of our brethren of the Clergy have been called to their great account, their pastoral staff broken, their flock given to another. They did not work for me, but for Him, the one Bishop and Shepherd of Souls ; and yet, as having shared with me the common burden of the cure of souls, I thank God for their labours, and desire that they may rest in peace, and "find mercy of the Lord in that day," and that His Blessing may abide continuously on their labours.

Indeed, since you last met your Bishop in Visitation, those solemn warnings have been very plain to this Diocese. Your Bishop, and one who had been formerly Bishop of this great See, as well as your Dean, have all been, I will not say taken from you, but withdrawn from your sight.

How much this Diocese owes to them, you, my brethren, well know by a grateful experience better than I can tell you. But of one, at least, you will pardon me if I attempt to speak, even one unworthy word.

"Great men" have received the title of their greatness, not merely from the attainment of an actual standard in the things which they have said or done, but from their relation to the persons and times in which they lived. They were men born for their day, gifted with the gifts required, and they used them. Such men are God's gifts, and they are great; both according to the Divine Standard, "they have done what they could," and also in the sight of men, by being greater than their fellows; they are great in what they do and say, even though their greatness be partly proved by enabling those who come after to do and say more than they themselves have done.

Bishop Wordsworth was consecrated Bishop of Lincoln on St. Matthias' Day, 1869. On the 8th of December in that same year the Vatican Council was assembled in St. Peter's Church at Rome. Bishop Wordsworth's Primary Visitation was in the following year, 1870. His Primary Charge[1] declares at once his position : he pronounces union with the Church of Rome on her present terms to be absolutely impossible, and yet he rejoices in the thought that many thoughtful persons in Roman Catholic countries are now being led by God's providence, which overrules evil for good, to examine the claims of the Roman Papacy, and to test them by Holy Scripture and Primitive Antiquity.[2]

These words, the "test of Holy Scripture and Primitive Antiquity," occurring as they do in Bishop Wordsworth's Primary Charge, might be taken as the motto of his Episcopate, and of his whole life. His work seemed eminently to be to maintain the Principles of the English Church on Scriptural and Primitive lines, to set out and maintain Anglican and Primitive Church Principles.[3]

But great as was Bishop Wordsworth's labour in, and knowledge of, Primitive and Anglican Theology, the work which renders him most singular among Students of Theology is his Commentary on the whole Bible. The very idea is exhausting ; and the courage, and patience, the varied knowledge, and spiritual insight, which enabled him to undertake and

---

[1] Primary Charge, 1870, p. 6.   [2] Primary Charge, p. 8.

[3] The very valuable little book, *Theophilus Anglicanus*, published as early as 1843, represents very much what he means ; it would be well if it were in the hands of (at least) the younger Clergy, and of Laymen who are anxious to know what Church Principles are.

accomplish so vast a work, make him great indeed ! How rich this Commentary is in Patristic and Anglican Theology would be better appreciated if the references were more frequently verified by his readers.

If it is not too great a presumption to offer a remark on such a work, I should desire to arrest the attention of, at least, my younger brethren, on one special feature of Bishop Wordsworth's Commentary—*its spiritual unity.* Unity of style is perhaps what we might expect in a Commentary from *one* hand ; but here there is *much more* than that: the hand was guided by a mind itself illuminated by the Holy Spirit of God, and it is the manifestation of the spiritual articulation, if I may use the word, the Divine connexion, by which the several Books of the Bible are linked as by golden links together, which renders this Commentary so precious to the seekers after Divine Truth ; for the Truth is Christ, and the object of revelation is to bring us to Christ, and in Christ to God. I have often wished that the Prolegomena of the several Books might be published in a separate volume by themselves, as a key to the right understanding of Holy Scripture ; I believe such a volume would be found to be in harmony with the Master's plan, when He opened the eyes of the Disciples, " that they might understand the Scriptures," and "beginning at Moses and all the prophets, expounded unto them, in all the Scriptures, the things concerning Himself."[4]

[4] S. Luke xxiv. 45-27.

ἐμοὶ δὲ ἀρχεῖά ἐστιν Ἰησοῦς Χριστός—S. Ign., Ep. ad Philad. viii.

Bishop Wordsworth, in his book on the interpretation of the Bible, has told us in his own words : [5] " If we wish to understand the Bible, we must not " " separate one portion of it from another ; we must " " endeavour to ascertain its sense by comparing " " spiritual things with spiritual . . . all parts " " of Scripture are dependent on one another, like " " joints in a well-organised body, or like parts of a " " beautiful building ; . . . we may not confine " " our attention to any one part of Scripture to the " " neglect of others, but must carefully consider the " " whole ; Almighty God has not revealed all truth in " " one book of Holy Scripture, but He has made one " " portion of Scripture ministerial and subsidiary to " " another : He has made the Book of Genesis to reflect " " light on the Book of Revelation, and He has made " " the Book of Revelation to illustrate the Book of " " Genesis."

Of Bishop Wordsworth's outward life, you, my brethren, do not need that I should speak : of his inner life, I cannot refrain, for my own edification, as well as for yours, from quoting the loving words of one who has a right to speak, his learned son, now, to our joy, Bishop of Salisbury. Preaching the Memorial Sermon in Lincoln Minster, his son said : " of his inner " life it is no secret to tell you that it was made up of " " constant, careful, prayer at stated times, and during " " many intervals of leisure throughout the day, for all "

---

[5] *Interpretation of the Bible*, by Christopher Wordsworth, 1861, pp. 108-118, cf. Note A.

" the work in which he was engaged, and all the "
" persons of whatever estate with whom he came in "
" contact, and of the constant study of Holy Scripture. "
" I believe that he never preached a sermon without "
" preparation before it on his knees, and private "
" prayer after it beforehe took off his robes (and that "
" throughout his life) that God would forgive its "
" imperfections, and prosper what was good and true "
" in it. So it was when coming from a Confirmation, "
" he knelt down at once in the house with the constant "
" companion of his journeys, whose prayers were so "
" closely linked with his, and prayed for those to whom "
" he had been administering the rite. It was the same "
" with Holy Scripture, he rarely, if ever, read the "
" Lessons, even in his own Chapel at Rischolme, "
" without first going through them and meditating on "
" them in private. Unless you could see the books "
" which we have the privilege of now turning over, "
" you could hardly believe the thoughtfulness and "
" minuteness with which all this side of his life was "
" marked " I make no apology for this long extract
nor yet for another from the same source, the
Sermon of his son.[6] It is from the Bishop's last words :
they show us, as the title of the sermon " Love and
Discipline " reminds us, that the Bishop was not a
stranger to suffering, but that he regarded it as from
the Lord, as from the hand of a loving Father. I quote
the words both because they are so characteristic of the
poetical and spiritual mind of their author, and because

[6] Memorial Sermon by John Wordsworth, March 29, 1885.

they may be a comfort to others in the hour of trial. "Amongst his last words (writes his son) *novissima verba*, I find in several forms this thought appearing, both in English and Latin, which he called the 'Law of suffering in nature'—the pruned Vine bearing purple clusters, the Grape crushed beneath the feet that tread the wine-vat, the Olive in the press, the Corn upon the threshing-floor, the Grass cut down and turning into fragrant hay, the Bread that supplies man's food when the corn is ground, the Lightning flashing from the darkest clouds, Gold tried and bright from the furnace, Gems that are brought to light and polished when rocks are broken up—all those were comforting images to him."

Let me conclude my unworthy memorial of my great predecessor by reminding you of the words in which he accepted me as his successor, "*Deo gratias*," and that he gave me his blessing. "He was in truth a great man for his learning, for his liberality, for his piety, and for his winning unworldly courtesy. He was and must ever remain great, even among the great men that during the past 800 years have been called to this ancient See."[7] I ask, brethren, for your constant prayers that I may follow him as he followed Christ.

When the Saviour ascended, the Angels warned the Disciples not to stand gazing up into Heaven, but to return to the place in which He had commanded

[7] Bishop of Lincoln's Address, Diocesan Conference, 1885.

them to remain; to wait until they knew what their work was to be, and until they had received power to do it. Of His own peculiar work, the Saviour could say "It is finished:" but *we* must look to begin more than we can finish here below.

> " That low man seeks a little thing to do,
>   Sees it, and does it :
>   This high man, with a great thing to pursue,
>   Dies ere he knows it." [8]

David, the man after God's own heart, *prepared* with all his might for the house of his God : but his son built it, enough for David that he had been entrusted with the Divine Pattern, and given strength to keep it to the end, and to hand it on for others to build by who should come after.

What is the special work then, which God has called me to do ? if I am not too presumptuous in speaking so definitely of myself in relation to God, I will say, I hope, if it be His Will, that my work may be to bring home to the hearts of the people, and especially of the poor, the blessings of the Church.

It seems to me that to this point God has been bringing us during these last thirty years. The last thirty, or five and thirty years, have been years of severe discipline for some of us ; severe, either in the suffering which we ourselves have suffered, or in the suffering which we have seen in others. The very foundations of the Faith have been assailed ; but, thanks be to God, they stand, for many of us, firmer than before ; or rather we stand firmer in our relation to them.

[8] Browning, A Grammarian's Funeral.

Two lines of thought have especially impressed themselves on my mind with regard to our belief in God, and I offer them for your consideration—one is that the evidence of our Faith is complex.

It is not in our power by the mere force of logic to arrive with perfect satisfaction at the conclusion—God is.[9] The subject is too great for such a method. We need rather considerations, lines of thought, than arguments ; we need the conjoint complex help of all our powers, physical, intellectual, moral, to enable us fully to rest in Him.[10] If it were not so, if we could have the power of knowing that He is, and Who He is, by the mere exercise of our minds, without turning our hearts and our bodies to His service, I fear some of us might be tempted to use our minds sufficiently to free ourselves from the misery of doubt, and give our hearts and our bodies to *another*.[1] Under

[9] I do not forget S. Anselm's Treatises : or Professor Mozley's clear and simple way of putting it, the mind demands "a cause with a stop in it"; nor the line of arguments lately given us by Dr. J. G. Cazenove. But for myself the conclusion from such reasoning has rather been "God must be than 'God is,'" and thus the result of the purely logical argument, if satisfactory to the intellect, still falls short of the "perfect satisfaction" which is desired.

Cf. *Dante Paradiso*, ch. xxiv., 131 :—

" E a tal creder non ho io pur prove
Fisice e metafisice, ma dalmi,
Anche la verita che quinci piove
Per Moisè, per profeti, e per salmi,
Per l'evangelio, e per voi che scriveste,
Poichè l' ardente Spirto vi fece almi."

[10] Cf. *Oxford House Papers*, No. viii., by T. B. Strong, p. 10. "The knowledge of God—which is man's highest knowledge—comes only through an effort of his whole humanity." Cf. Bishop Ellicott's *Lectures on the Being of God.*—S.P.C.K.

[1] Ps. xvi. 4.—So I remember Dr. Pusey saying in the last year of his Lectures, "it does not say explicitly another God, but 'another,' anything than God."

the discipline of doubt, God has been leading us to lay hold on Him with all our powers, and thus has brought us again to see, with a new clearness, that our reasonable service is to offer to Him ourselves, our souls, and our bodies. You will easily see, my brethren, what a wide field of work this opens before us with our people ; even the perfecting of their several faculties, that they may rest more completely in God : what scope there is here for physical, intellectual, moral, and spiritual progress :[2] what need of reverent and loving labour to watch and train and perfect the several faculties in man's mysterious nature ; what need to put away all envy and jealousy of each other, and with united efforts each to contribute what he may to accomplish for his brother this complex, this blessed result. God is the end of Man, not of his mind only, but of his heart and will : nay, the Apostle tells us, the " body is for the Lord."[3]

The other line of thought which has impressed itself upon me in these last years is that faith, after all, is a gift from God. It is not the mere sum of probabilities, conjectures, or reasonings of any kind, but, as Bishop Pearson has expressed it, " Faith is the gift of God, not only in the object, but also in the act."[4] " By grace are ye saved through faith ; and

[2] This shows the true importance of Athletic Societies, Literary Institutes, Schools of Art, etc., Guilds, and Retreats.

[3] 1 Cor. vi. 13.

[4] Bishop Pearson On the Creed, art. viii., p. 387 ; cf. also p. 388, " As the increase and perfection, so the original, or initiation of faith is from the Spirit of God, not only by an external proposal in the word, but by an internal illumination in the soul."

that not of yourselves ; it is the gift of God :"[5] a gift, be it remembered, which is never denied to those who seek it with true lowliness and sincerity of heart.

And yet I think Bishop Pearson's definition of Faith in his first Article led me more or less to a dangerous line of thought, where he speaks of Faith as an "act or habit of the understanding ;[6]" as the "assent unto that which is credible as credible." This is true, no doubt : but Faith is more than an act of the understanding : it implies the action of the affections and of the Will, the exercise of all those inner powers of our being which the Hebrews called the Heart. So again, I think, in the atmosphere of the last thirty years, even the golden sentence of Bishop Butler has been dangerous "To us probability is the guide of Life." We all know what the great Bishop meant ; we do act to the death on evidence that is but probable, in temporal matters, and we ought not to refuse to do so in matters of religion (for religion is a practical thing ;[7]) because we have not another kind of evidence which satisfies the vanity of intellect better. Sailer has expressed the truth of our position very well. "We require," he says, "a surrender,"[8] an "acceptance," and

[5] Eph. ii. 8.   [6] Bishop Pearson, art. i., 2.

[7] Cf. Bishop Butler's *Analogy*, pt. ii., cap. viii., p. 279. "Religion is a practical thing."

[8] Sailer, Bishop of Ratisbon, *Grundlehren der Religion*, iv., 55—83 ; Aufzugeben, annehmen, glauben.

I am indebted to Dr. Döllinger for my knowledge of Sailer's Works. They are very simple, and perhaps others might not care for them, but he held his ground through all the troubles of the French Revolution and the influence of Voltaire, and threw himself head and heart into the work of helping the young Students in Germany ; and I am grateful for his many writings, not scientifically, perhaps, very important, but evidently united, and fired by something of a spiritual genius.

"Faith." This need of a gift to enable us fully to believe in God brings out with a new clearness the fundamental importance of Revelation, the inestimable value of our Bible even in relation to Theism. It is one of the results of these last years, that, by the comparative study of Religions, we have seen how hardly one, if one, of all the Philosophies and Religions of the world has been able to establish in its purity the belief in One God.[9] If the present learned Bishop of Salisbury has told us that Theism is implied in the ordinary religious language of the Heathen world, we must remember how he has added that this is but as a sort of quiet back-ground of belief waiting to be called into actuality at the approach of light. Nature (our Archbishop has lately told us) suspects a God, but cannot prove it.[1] Without the aid of Revelation the Apostle has told us men are but seeking God if haply they might feel after him and find Him;[2] just as we may be conscious of the presence of a person in a dark room, though who he may be, or where, we cannot tell.

My brethren, you will easily see with what zeal and enthusiasm, we should strive to make the Scriptures known to our people, lest they should lose the very knowledge of God. Earnestly as I would exhort you to have faith in the " unapparent capabilities " of our people for social and political progress, yet still more earnestly do I desire to warn you that no mere

---

[9] Present Bishop of Salisbury's *Bampton Lectures.*

[1] *The Seven Gifts*, Archbishop Benson, p. 228. "The conscious God, whom nature suspects but cannot prove." Cp. Ro. i. 20.

[2] Acts xvii. 27.

progress in secular education or political power will
teach men the full knowledge of God. The experience
of the world teaches us that there may be wealth, and
power, and art, without the knowledge of the true God.

Consider then, dear brethren, whether we are not
allowing our people individually, and our nation col-
lectively, to run great risk from the thoughtless
neglect of their Bible.

I have ventured to speak to you of these elementary
truths because some of us have learnt under the
dicipline of doubt to consider again these first principles
of our Faith, and, through God's mercy, the result has
been, to many, a closer and more real relation to their
old belief; and though I would not have you thought-
lessly disturb the minds of the people by unnecessary
speculative questions, yet I believe we might do them
good service, and help them to a firmer and more
living faith, if we spent more time and labour in
bringing each separate soul to the prayerful consideration of these fundamental truths, instead of confining
ourselves merely to practical exhortations; our people
need *exercising in religious thought* as well as ourselves;
they need S. Bernard's rule,[3] "get time to think,"*vacare
considerationi;* they need the warning of the Psalmist,
" be still then and know that I am God."

But if these last years have been years of discipline
with regard to our belief in God, hardly less have
they been so with regard to belief in ourselves. There
have been times during these last thirty years when

[3] S. Bernard de Consideratione.

it has seemed to some as though the brilliant and beneficial progress of natural science would cause the study of morals to be like silver in the days of Solomon, "nothing accounted of:" nay more, it has almost seemed as if morals would be scientifically destroyed, and be shown to lack a rational basis. It is in a sense a new gift, for which we ought with all thankfulness to acknowledge the responsibility, that this is so no longer. Ethics have again a position among scientific realities.[4]

But here again God has brought us through the darkness into clearer light : and on two points I would venture to ask your consideration, for the sake of your people (for it is for them that I am speaking).

 1. We need a true standard of morals.

 2. We need more careful cultivation of the
   moral life.

By a true standard of morals I mean the Christian standard. It is one of the points which have been made clearer to us during these last years, that we have made so little of *Christian* Ethics. While the Universities were by statute Christian it was assumed that their members were instructed in the principles of the Christian Faith, and that the deficiencies of Heathen Ethics would be at once supplied ; but when it was no longer necessary for the members of the Universities to be Christians, and men studied Pagan philosophy independently of, or as a substitute for, the

[4] I cannot help here expressing, as an Oxford man, how inestimable a debt we owe to the work and writings of the late Professor of Moral Philosophy, T. H. Green.

Christian Faith, then we saw our weakness, and felt the need of considering afresh what the moral nature of man ought to be under the perfect example of our Lord and Saviour Jesus Christ, and with the new powers which flow to us through His Incarnation. The doctrine of perfection, which formed an attractive part of John Wesley's preaching, could never be satisfactorily dealt with by a Church which was content to base its moral teaching chiefly on the four cardinal virtues, and to illustrate them from the writings of the heathen : though it must be confessed that it would have been well if all those who wished to go on unto perfection had kept these four stones among the foundations of their more ambitious building.

We need to bring more vividly before our people the pattern of our Lord's Life, and of His Life in His Saints, to make them dissatisfied with the too common standard of self-measurement and mutual comparison, and to fire them with the true ambition of being like Him.

And if we need a true standard of Ethics so do we need more careful cultivation of the moral powers. I do not forget that the great moral life of humanity is progressing, and that we are in some ways better than those who lived before us. But to those who have the perception of moral phenomena, it is sheer misery to see the needless waste which is going on all around us for want of due cultivation. Here again we have a new responsibility from the example which has been set us in our day by the students of natural science. What reverent, loving, labour do they bestow to discern the ways of a worm or a plant! What constant persevering efforts will they make with the microscope to see into the nature and relations, if they will not call them the causes, of things! And what are we doing, my brethren, which will in any way bear comparison with these labours, to find out the ways of our people, to know, that is, what is in man, what labour we need to surmount the barriers of class, and wealth, and education? How hopeless it often is to speak of moral perfection with such reckless surroundings! How unscientific to expect to make man act rightly without studying the motives of his actions! We have indeed a noble field of work before us—the perfecting of the English people—but before we can hope to succeed we must study the problem more.

You see, brethren, what is in my mind, and in my heart; it is a practical matter: it is how to bring the Truth to the people, that in the Truth they may be made free, and in this freedom draw nearer to one another and to God. For this is the perfection of man, to love God, and to love his fellow-men. And this brings me back to the point from which I have so long diverged, where I ventured to state what, in submission to the Divine will, I hoped, with your aid, might be my work—to bring home to the hearts of the people, and especially of the poor, the blessings of the Church.

If the practical question before us is: "How to bring the truth to the people," I answer, in and by

the Church. If the practical question is, " How are
the people to reach this intended moral perfection,"
I reply again, in and by the Church. It was for these
purposes that our Blessed Lord founded His Kingdom
on earth ; that in it man might know the Father and
His Son Jesus Christ, and be a partaker of His merits,
and be truly sanctified by the indwelling of the Holy
Ghost. It was for this that He entrusted to His
Church the two-fold ministry of the Word and Sacraments. In the Church the essential truths of salvation
were to be preserved and taught. The Church was
to be the living instrument of our sanctification ; in
the Church and by the Church He would give us the
sanctifying power of His Holy Spirit. In the Church
He instituted the Sacraments as the special means
whereby we might become partakers of His Divine
nature through the operation of the Holy Spirit.
The object of the Church, the end for which
it was founded, is expressed by S. Paul, " He
gave some, apostles ; and some, prophets ; and
some, evangelists ; and some, pastors and teachers ;
for the perfecting of the Saints, for the work of the
ministry, for the edifying of the Body of Christ : till
we all come in the unity of the faith, and of the knowledge of the Son of God, unto a perfect man, unto
the measure of the stature of the fulness of Christ :
that we henceforth be no more children tossed to and
fro, and carried about with every wind of doctrine,
by the sleight of men, and cunning craftiness, whereby

B

they lie in wait to deceive ; but speaking the truth
in love, may grow up unto Him in all things, which is
the Head, even Christ : from whom the whole body
fitly joined together and compacted by that which
every joint supplieth, according to the effectual working
in the measure of every part, maketh increase of the
body unto the edifying of itself in love."[5]

In other words the great ends for which the Church
of Christ was in God's mercy founded are the restoration of man to himself, to his God, and to his fellow
man, in love, *i.e.*, in God.

And here, my brethren, I feel I need to offer you
an apology for repeating truths with which you have been
so long familiar.   My apology is that I do this not for
your own sake but for the sake of the poor and un-
instructed, who are our common responsibility.   Bear
with me then if I repeat what you know ; bearing in
mind who He was Who at the great crisis of the world's
history "spake the same words."[6]   Indeed there need be
no mental tautology in the repetition of pregnant words.
Our danger, in a day of cheap printing and constant
speaking, lies rather the other way.   We pass on to
new words too quickly, we pay too little attention to
the responsibility of speech, and the depth and unity of
truth.

But if I offer a sincere apology for this repetition,
" is there not a cause " ?   Are all our people intelligent
members of the Church ?   Does the phrase, " Church
of England," mean that every Englishman is an

[5] Eph. iv. 11—16.   [6] St. Mark xiv. 39.

instructed Churchman ?   Is it not a common complaint
amongst the Clergy that even their good people have
but a poor idea of what the Church is?   Are not
Church principles very often a "Missing Link"?
And one reason of this is not hard to find.   It comes
partly from the very fragmentary instruction which
has been given on this great subject to most of us of
the Clergy.

At Oxford, lately, a School of Theology has been
established which has done, and I trust will do
increasingly, by God's blessing, a good work for the
Church ; but what does it reveal as to the amount of
definite Theological instruction which is given to
English Students of Theology with regard to the
Church ?   On the being and nature of God, on Revelation, on the relation of man's natural powers to the
Holy Spirit, on Grace, on special Forms of Christian
Worship, on the History of the Church from the
earliest to the present time, on these, and on some
kindred subjects, there is now excellent instruction
given.[7]   And yet the Church is not given as a separate
subject to be studied in relation to the Incarnation,
in its origin, object, organization, and essential charac-
teristics.   I do not say that such knowledge is not to
be obtained, but it is gathered indirectly, and not in
that definite and scientific form which, at least for
beginners, is generally helpful.   The truth is, that in
this matter we suffer still from the want which Bishop

[7] May I suggest to any of my younger brethren that the Syllabus of Books
recommended for this School at Oxford, contains one of the best schemes for
Theological reading that the Church of England has had for many years ?

Pearson felt, which he pointed out and hoped to remedy when he was appointed to teach Theology in Cambridge, and determined to write a "Summa Theologiæ ex sententia Doctoris in Ecclesia Anglicana tradita."[8] If we ourselves, my Reverend Brethren, have received but irregular instruction on this great subject, it is not improbable that our teaching may not always have possessed that simplicity and fulness which are the marks of thorough knowledge, and which our people require.

That there is need for more definite instruction as to the nature and privileges of the Church, we might infer again from the Committee which has been lately appointed by the Lower House of Convocation of this Province, to draw up certain questions on the Church, to be added to the Church Catechism. This Committee is, indeed, an acknowledgement that our poor people need more help in this matter.

If the want of more instruction may form part of my apology, so also, perhaps, may the opportunity which the present circumstances afford. The discipline of doubt under which God has been pleased to bring us during these last thirty years has, by His mercy, brohght many into clearer relation with the old utruts. The questions of the Personality of God, of man's Personality, of the union between God and man in Christ, have led men to consider with a new reality how this is to be ; to ask, since they are to

[8] Cf. Bishop Pearson's *Minor Works*, vol. i., p. lvii., by E. Churton, and Bishop Pearson's 2nd Lecture, "De existentia Dei." "More plane scholastico sed secundum principia reformata."

be saved by Christ, which is the way of Salvation that Christ has appointed for them : and this has, I thank God, brought not a few to the old position of the early Christians : that as Christ discloses the mind of the Father, so the Church tells us the mind of Christ : that the Church is the Body of Christ, and that to be in Christ we must be in His Body. Men's minds have been purified by the suffering of doubt to see these truths more clearly than before, and subjects which had little interest before the troubles came are now eagerly attended to.

I need not remind you of the recent interest given to the Church Question from its connexion with the State. The political circumstances of the present time give us an especial opportunity to teach the people both what the Church is not, and what she is.

But I believe that my apology is sufficient, and that it is rather the difficulty of doing it, than want of conviction of the need for its being done, that keeps us from bringing Church Principles more clearly and fully before the people.

Let me mention what some of the difficulties are— First, there is still the confusion between Catholic and Roman Catholic. Men fear when we speak about the Church, that we mean 'to assert some special privi- leges of the Clergy ; that we are preferring authority to reason ; that all individual judgment will be crushed, and that the end of Church teaching must be submission to the Bishop of Rome. We must recog- nise, and do our best to remove this fear, and let it be clearly known, and understood, that while we desire earnestly reunion with the Church of Rome, *if* she will first bring herself into doctrinal union with the Primitive Church, yet we cannot accept her new additions to the Faith ; and though we would grant to the See of Rome her ancient primacy, yet we cannot accept it as it is now offered, transformed into a *quasi* sacramental Headship.

Another more subtle difficulty lies in the apparent paradox in the use of media. The soul is jealous of any interference between itself and God. Possessing powers for the enjoyment through eternity of the unveiled vision of God, the soul is impatient of the mediatorial kingdom ; it feels the restraint of times, and places, and persons ; it longs for the communion with God and with the saints in Heaven where the Lord is the temple." This fear of interference between the soul and its God makes the soul jealous of Sacraments, of Priesthood, of Creeds, of a Church, even in some cases of a Bible.

This jealousy for union with God is worthy of the greatest respect and consideration, for it speaks of a great past, and is a pledge of a still greater future. But it needs Fatherly instruction and correction. We are on our way back again to God, but it is as those who have fallen from God, and we need the discipline of times, and places, and persons, if we are to inherit the fulness of the freedom that is prepared for us, and to follow the Lamb whithersoever He goeth. We need

" Rev. xxi. 22.

to consider the apparent paradox that by separation and limitation God is reconciling the world back again to Himself. G‹d loved all the world, yet He chose one nation to be His own. God loved the Chosen People, but He chose one particular Tribe to minister to Holy Things. He loved all the sons of Levi, but chose the Family of Aaron to be His Priests. God was in all the world, yet He chose Jerusalem to be the City where He would dwell. In the language of Scripture, God deviseth means that His banished be not expelled from Him.[1] What the soul requires to know is that there is no union between God and man, except through Him Who is both Man and God ; that in the Church. and by the Sacraments, we are made Partakers of Him ; that the Church is His Body, that as members of His Church we are incorporated into Him, and in Him are reconciled back again to God. The Sacraments, the Priesthood, the Creeds, the Bible itself, the Church, are not barriers between the soul and God, but the divinely appointed media for re-union : for as Hooker says, " faith in the Sacraments is part of belief."

Another great hindrance to the definite inculcation of Church principles is the presence of Non-conformists amongst us. Our reverence and love for their zeal and religious efforts, our unwillingness to disturb the peace and goodwill which often exists between us and them ; this kindly feeling hinders us from the truer kindness of speaking the truth. On both sides there

[1] II Sam. xiv. 14.

is often need of more knowledge, and of that quiet trustfulness in the truth which comes with knowledge. All we desire is the full and patient statement of the truth; and then we may trust to the working of the Holy Spirit to bring conviction in His own time.

On our part, my Reverend Brethren, I would suggest a more thorough acquaintance with the history and tenets of the different forms of Dissent. In such study we should assume that no body of men will band themselves together upon the basis of error as error, but either because they hold, or think they hold, some elements of truth not recognized by others. Our endeavour should be to see what those elements of truth are which have so attracted them as to cause them to separate from us, and then to show them how they may be had in the Church in greater perfection, being there held in harmony with other truths.

Too often, it must be confessed, it has been the neglect of some truth on the part of the Church which has provoked an exaggerated reaction; and the neglected truth has become the watch-word of a sect. No one can doubt that the great spiritual movement, whose birth-place is in this county, arose from a desire for higher personal holiness, the desire to make sure that religion was a personal thing; from a sense of the need of more help in the religious life, the help of system and discipline. It was this which led to the establishment of a system of classes graduated according to the spiritual capacity of the individual members, so that each might be brought to God, and led on to perfection. In all this there is surely much truth which the Church should well consider, and provide accordingly.

Another great difficulty in teaching Church principles to the uneducated arises from their ignorance of Church History. To appeal at once to Church History is too often unmeaning and useless. We must seek for some lines of thought, by which the system of the Church can be brought before the people without requiring a knowledge of Church History ; and we should seek for new ways by which Church History may be taught.

Two or three such lines of thought have suggested themselves to me, which I desire to mention.

1. First there is the consideration of the Church as a society. The recent extension of the franchise has led many of our agricultural poor to see that they have capacities for wider and higher relations than they thought. They can see now that they not only may have an interest in themselves, but in the welfare of their fellow-countrymen ; and not only so, but, as nations are interlaced with nations, national politics they can see must have a European, and even a wider interest : and thus an individual may see now that he has an interest, not only in the welfare of his fellow-countrymen, but in the brotherhood of man. It is greatly to be hoped that the new opportunities for local government will enable people to rise higher above all local selfishness, and self-interest, and regard these

opportunities as initial spheres of education for the discharge of higher political responsibilities. The thoughtless and unintelligent discharge of local government has often, I fear, led to great waste of opportunities for political education.

The same is true in the government of the Church. It should be the ambition of every Church Layman to contribute something to the common good; the intelligent discharge of the duties of Vestry-man, Sidesman, and Churchwarden might lead on to a share in the Meeting of the Rural Deanery, in the Diocesan Conference. and now in the Provincial House of Laymen.

The Church, as a society, with rules and laws, supplies the need of external help which even the Heathen moralist declared man to have—leading us to the conclusion that man reaches his individual happiness and perfection by acting in union with his fellow men, and that the human will needs the external assistance of rules and laws to enable it to carry out the principles which reason and conscience approve. We need to be placed in a society, we need a rule of life. It was this line of thought, you will remember, which led Aristotle when he had finished the Ethics to write the Politics. Ethics, personal morality, should be regarded as the Vestibule to Politics, the principles of the life of nations

If our people now see that they have capacities for relations and powers of which they were hitherto not aware, is it not an opportunity for asking them to consider the still wider relations and higher capacities which lie in them and around them in their relation to the Catholic, or Universal Church ?

2. Another consideration is the Scriptural evidence for the Church.

This we should try to set before our people, not by quoting one or two individual texts, but rather by showing that the idea of the Church, as a Society, with definite organization and means of grace is Scriptural, *i.e.,* according to the revealed mind of God.

We should point out how before the Law, and under the Law, and in the Gospel, God's Will has been to use the media of times, and persons, and even things inanimate, for the restoration of man. We should point out how to preach Jesus, in Apostolic times, implied the Sacrament of Baptism which Jesus had appointed.[2]

We should show them how the Scriptures speak of the Church as the "Body" of Christ, as the "Spouse" and "Bride" of Christ, and therefore that the Church was meant to be *one.* We should show them how Christ added to the Church such as were being saved : how, as Bishop Pearson says,[3] "Christ never appointed two ways to Heaven, nor did He build a Church to save some, and make another institution for *other* men's salvation": how, as Bishop Taylor[4] has said, "There is, in ordinary, no way to

[2] Acts viii. 35-38.   [3] Acts ii. 41.   Bishop Pearson, *Creed*, art. ix.

[4] Bishop Taylor, *On Repentance*, vol. ix. p. 258 : Wordsworth, *Theoph. Angl.* p. 26.

Heaven but by serving God in the way which He hath commanded us by His Son ; that is, in the way of the Church which is His Body, of which He is the Prince and Head." And all this is but the extension of that same principles of mediation upon which when the Son of Man took upon Him to deliver man He did not abhor the Virgin's womb. The instrument by which He then executed the Will which He came to do was that Body which was prepared for Him ; that soul which was made an offering for sin ; that spirit which, when He had finished His work, He commended unto His Father's hands.

We must show them moreover how the Old Testament ministries of Prophet, Priest, and King are not wholly exhausted in their meaning by the coming of Him who is *the* Prophet, Priest, and King.

We must explain Scripture as the Early Fathers did both in the East and West; and explain the Pastoral Epistles as relating to the Christian Ministry as they had it, and as we now have it, with Bishops, Priests, and Deacons.

We must tell them, as the Early Fathers did, (even St. Cyprian and St. Irenæus) how the lesson of schism in the histories of Korah, Nadab, and Jeroboam is a warning to those who break away from the Divinely 'appointed Ministry of the Christian Church.

We must show them how the greatness of their own position as "Priests and Kings" no more does away with a definite Christian Priesthood than it did away with the Aaronic Priesthood, when the words were first spoken under the Law, or any more than it does away with the rights of Kings in a Christian land. We may tell them, if we think it necessary, as S. Augustine told his Catechumens, that there is an element of *temporary imitation and discipline* in all this, for the Kingdom of God of which we are speaking is the Kingdom in its militant condition. We may remind them that there will come a time when this Militant Kingdom will be delivered up to the Father, and then we shall no longer need this ministry of men, neither the Sacraments, nor the Scriptures, nor the latter petitions at least of the Lord's Prayer. But if we tell them this it must not be to flatter any spirit of self-righteous independence of the means of grace which God has provided for them, but rather to warn them against impatience in accepting the conditions of the Militant Kingdom. The Church is the ark which God has builded for our safety, and in which we are being brought unto the Haven where we would be.

3. There is another consideration which might be made of far more practical value than it often is, I mean the consideration of the clause in the Apostles' Creed, "I believe in the Holy Catholic Church"; and in the Nicene Creed, "I believe one Catholic and Apostolic Church."

Many of our people would be shocked at the imputation of rejecting, or mutilating the Creeds, who, nevertheless, do not give themselves time to consider what they mean when they say, I believe in "One

Holy Catholic Apostolic Church." And yet, every child that is brought to Church to be Christened, or, having been privately Christened, is publicly received into the Congregation, does, by its Godfathers and Godmothers, promise to believe the Articles of the Creed, and Godparents are admonished to take care that the child shall be taught it. And again, at the close of life, in the Office for the Visitation of the Sick, the question is to be asked among the fundamental articles of the soul's belief, "dost thou believe in the Holy Catholic Church?" Twice, every day, the Church requires, at least, of her Clergy, this statement of our belief to be made, and as often as we celebrate the Holy Communion. This we all know, but do all who accept these facts, practically realise what they involve? Is it not true that on this article of the Creed the teaching has often been, from different causes, short and vague? Have we not much work yet to do before all those who accept the Creed shall individually, and with a practical intelligence, accept this clause in the sense in which it was understood when inserted in the Creeds by the Fathers of the Primitive Church? What the meaning of the Primitive Church was we can see by the position of this clause in the Creeds. It follows the clause which expresses our belief in the Holy Ghost, and it tells us that the means of grace and salvation are to be obtained in and through the Church; that the Church is the present manifestation of the power of Christ, the divinely appointed sphere for the operations of the Holy Spirit. And so the four great wants of man, expressed in the four following clauses,—holiness : "the forgiveness of sins,"—the certainty of a continuing personality : "the resurrection of the body" —the rest and bliss of sinless love : "the Communion of Saints,"—and that for ever and ever : "the life everlasting,"—these four great wants of man, we are given to understand, are to be had in, or through, the Church ; " per Sanctam Ecclesiam," as it was sometimes expressed.

Let me, for the sake of your poor people, remind you of the words of my learned predecessor, Bishop Wordsworth.

"What," he asks, "was the judgment of the Primitive Church upon this point ?" And his reply is. "It declared in its Creeds, that the means of grace and salvation can only be obtained in the Church ; that remission of sins can only be had there ; that the Sacrament of the Eucharist, the graces of the Spirit, and the Word of God, pure and incorrupt, can be received only in the Church ; that prayer can only be offered up acceptably to God, and that benediction can only be received in Communion with the Church of Christ. ' Nulla salus, nisi in Ecclesia ' was the concurrent language of all antiquity ; and in the words of S. Cyprian and of S. Augustine, ' Nemo potest habere Deum Patrem, qui non habet Ecclesiam Matrem.' " [5] Such language, I know, at once excites feelings of opposition, as if the liberty of God, and the law of

[5] *Theoph. Ang.*, ch. iv., pp. 28, 29.

charity, were being broken; but it need not be so Because we believe that " Whoso hath the Son hath life, and whoso hath not the Son hath not life," we do not necessarily condemn those to whom the Name of the Son has never been made known; we pass no judgment on the world before Christ came, nor on those portions of the world which remain, alas! heathen at the present day; nor yet upon the irresponsibly or invincibly ignorant or on the imbecile. Man's responsibilities vary with his privileges: Christ's merits we know are infinite. " Every one shall be dealt equitably with "; all will be judged by God, and " God is love." [6] Indeed the thought of the heathen and the ignorant may rather suggest thoughts of fear and warning for ourselves than for them, unless we pray for them, and regard it as a part of our Christian duty to do what we can to make known to them the blessings of the Gospel of Christ. We must accept the responsibilities, as well as the privileges, of the Church.

4. There is one more consideration on which I desire to ask your attention in relation to our people and their belief in the Church, and that is Church History. Our difficulty is very great. The Church was intended to be the Divinely appointed instrument for teaching the people, and we have now, for the most part, to teach our people to listen to their teacher; to teach them who their teacher is, that they may trust her, that they may " hear the Church." And

[6] Bishop Butler's *Analogy*, pt. ii., ch. vi., *Theoph. Ang.*, p. 31.

yet we may be sure, as she is the appointed teacher of the people, we shall, in the end, teach them best if we teach them in God's way. As to many persons their knowledge of Church History must, of course, be very small. And yet might we not, if we freed ourselves from sloth and despair, do something more than we have done in the matter? The efforts and progress in technical knowledge in other sciences are very great; new efforts are being constantly made to break up the great mass of the knowable, so that, according to capacity and aptitude, each may receive something.

In every village there would be *some* who might make *some* progress in this matter.

The teachers in our day schools, our pupil teachers, our Sunday-school teachers—might make some progress; and, here and there, one or two of the more educated parishioners. I hope with the assistance of the Diocesan Board of Education to establish a scheme for higher religious education such as has been lately established in the Diocese of Oxford; a part of which is to deliver Lectures on Church History in different centres in the Diocese, and to offer questions for examination to any who may desire such assistance. Something again, I think, might be done by creating a *local* interest in Church History. Several Diocesan Histories have been written in the last few years : might we not advance a step further and obtain, if not separate histories of each Parish, yet histories of each Rural Deanery made up from the histories of each separate Parish, as far as they could contribute? Such histories might form from time to time part of the Parish Magazine, and would be read with interest by some, at least, in each separate neighbourhood.

I cannot help adding here that we might, I think, do more in keeping the Dedication Festival of the Parish Church. No doubt such festivals have degenerated into mere secular feasts, and we must be content with simple results, and results of a very mixed character, from such an effort; but I believe the sympathies of the young might be largely drawn towards the Church by such means; while the aged would enter more into the Services of the day, and understand, at least in some degree, what a blessing it is to have a Church.

For yourselves, my Reverend Brethren, I hardly like to presume to suggest anything, when you may be so much more able to do it than I am. I will, however, offer two more suggestions :—Might not our teaching about the Church have been more strong and definite if we had seen more clearly the gradual growth of the errors of the Church of Rome ? Have we not lost members of our Church to the Church of Rome, because they were so imperfectly instructed in the answers to modern Roman claims, and has not this want of instruction partly arisen from our ignorance of the years in which Roman error has grown up ? The usual knowledge of Church History required of the Clergy of the Church of England has been of the first three or four centuries, and of the Reformation, which leaves a blank of a thousand or twelve hundred years, I know that the Modern History

School at the Universities has done much to remedy this danger, but might we not improve? The other suggestion I venture to offer is to invite your attention to a double responsibility which rests upon us in this Diocese, one indeed in common with the whole Church—I mean the re-assurance we have lately had given us by the learned labours of the Bishop of Durham of the genuineness of the Ignatian Epistles. This should make us consider again how necessary the three sacred orders are, if we would enjoy the full blessings of the Church, and a valid Eucharist. This is certainly the teaching of St. Ignatius,[7] and it is in harmony with the teaching of our own Ordinal, " It is evident unto all men diligently reading the Holy Scriptures and Ancient Authors, that from the Apostles' time there have been these three orders of Ministers in Christ's Church : Bishops, Priests, and Deacons."[7] "We require you, says Hooker, to find out one Church upon the face of the whole earth that hath not been ordered by Episcopal regiment since the time that the blessed Apostles were here conversant."[8]

If we need the study of the middle ages to teach us the origin of the Roman additions to the old faith, we need the study of the early centuries to save us from using the word 'Church' of Organizations,

---

[7] Cf. Ep. ad Smyrn. C viii. ἐκείνη βεβαία εὐχαριστία ἡγείσθω ἡ ὑπὸ τὸν ἐπίσκοπον οὖσα ἢ ᾧ ἂν αὐτὸς ἐπιτρέψῃ . . . . . οὐκ ἐξόν ἐστιν χωρὶς τοῦ ἐπισκόπου οὔτε βαπτίζειν οὔτε ἀγάπην ποιεῖν.

Bishop Lightfoot's note on the last words is " the ἀγάπη must include the Eucharist."

[7] Preface to Ordination Services, Prayer Book Service.   [8] Preface iv. 1.

for which it was never used in primitive times. In this Diocese we have a special responsibility from the writings which have been left us by your late revered Bishop. I will ask you, in this my first Charge since he has been taken from you, to look again, and yet again, at the Patristic and Anglican evidence which he has given us on the organization and privileges of the Church in that small but pregnant book, to which I have already referred—" Theophilus Anglicanus ".

Let it be a labour of grateful love that we try to follow up that Patristic teaching, to enrich it by further reading, to make it our own by prayerful meditation ; and then to labour unceasingly, and by every available means, to make that teaching known to the people. For this, my brethren, I earnestly invite your renewed assistance, that we may bring home to the people the blessings of the Church.[9] That is, in other words, let us show how the Church in her ministry of the Word and Sacraments provides for the three great wants of man :—

Truth—Holiness—Peace.

I will conclude these simple suggestions for a renewed effort to instruct our people in the doctrines

---

[9] What those blessings are Bishop Wordsworth has well set out in his chapters on the Privileges of the Church. *Theoph. Angl.*, pt. i. ch. vi.-xvi.
    1—The Word of God.
    2—The Right Interpretation of the Word of God.
    3—The Administration of the Sacraments by a Lawful Ministry.
    4—Discipline, Power of the Keys.
    5—Absolution.
    6—Sacerdotal Intercession and Benediction.
    7—Set Forms of Public Prayer.

of the Church, by some words from a treatise by an Eastern (a Russian) Bishop.[10]

1—The Lord Jesus has founded His Church that that in it we might be born again. We ought therefore, to show her the love and obedience of children.

2—The Lord Jesus has charged His Church to teach men His loving doctrine. We, therefore, should receive her teaching as from the Holy Spirit.

3—The Lord Jesus has intrusted to the Church the Sacraments and Divine Offices for the sanctification of men. We should accept and use them with fitting reverence.

4—The Lord Jesus has appointed the Church to guide and strengthen men in a life of piety. We should loyally follow and obey her rules and laws.

5—The Lord Jesus has appointed in His Church a distinction between the pastor and the flock. We should receive these different gifts as determined by His Will.

6—The Church of Christ is *One.* Therefore we should preserve the Spirit of Unity in the bond of peace.

7—The Church of Christ is *Holy.* Therefore we should strive to keep ourselves fitting members of the Body of Which Christ is Himself the Head.

[10] Macaire. *Théologie Dogmatique Orthodoxe,* P. iii , s. ii., ch. i.

8—The Church of Christ is *Catholic*, or universal. Therefore it is for the whole world, and our love should be for all mankind.

9—The Church of Christ is *Apostolic*. Therefore we should stand firm in the Faith, being built on the foundation of the Apostles and Prophets, united in Jesus Christ, who is Himself the Chief Corner Stone.—EPH. ii. 20.

From the reconsideration of these general principles let us now turn our attention to the present condition of our Diocese.

1. First let me offer both to you, my brethren of the Clergy, and to you my brethren of the Laity, my grateful thanks for the kind forbearance, and ready assistance, which you have shown me during the past eighteen months. I accept it as your answer to that touching appeal made to you, on my behalf, in our Minster by your late Bishop's son: " Will you not, for your part, who loved my father, do him this best, this greatest kindness, to transfer your love and generous forbearance, your respect and loyal confidence, to the successor whom God, I believe, has sent in answer to his earnest and anxious prayers ? "[1]

It is not possible for me to give my thanks individually to all of you to whom my thanks are due, but you will expect that I should make some special reference to the Bishop of Nottingham, whose valuable services as Bishop Suffragan, (I say it with regret for

[1] Memorial Sermon by John Wordsworth, M.A., 1885, p. 9.

your sake, as well as for my own,) I have not felt able to continue, now that the Diocese has been relieved of more than one half of its population by the creation of the See of Southwell. I am thankful, however, to assure you that the Bishop of Nottingham will both continue to aid me by his services in the Archdeaconry of Stow, and in those many known, and unknown, generous ways by which he has assisted the work of the Church in this Diocese for so many years.

My thanks are due to the Dean and Chapter of our Cathedral Church for the readiness with which they have accorded to me the special use of the Minster for Ordinations, Confirmations, and at other times, as well as for their continued readiness to aid me by their counsel and loving sympathy. I trust that my removal of the Episcopal residence back again to the site of the Old Palace of St. Hugh, so as to be able to live amongst them, may be the outward sign of a real and increasing union in brotherly love, and united labour for the Diocese.

To the Rural Deans I wish indeed that I could give my thanks individually for the readiness with which all were willing to continue their unremunerated office on my appointment to this See, or to accept the office as vacancies occurred.

I am aware that the new Pluralities Act makes new demands on the self-sacrificing sincerity, and Christian tact, of the Rural Dean ; but I cannot but believe, if we remember Whom we serve, that grace will be given. I take this opportunity of returning my thanks for the record of your Chapter proceedings which many of you have been good enough to send me. I observe in some cases that the Laity attend; might not this attendance be increased, and be made a valuable means of enlisting the interest of the Laity in the Church's work?

And to you, my brethren of the Laity, I offer my thanks in the Name of Him, Whose we are, and Whom we serve, for your self-denying services for His Church. To Him you look for praise and reward, and not to me. I trust that no change in the financial position of the office will prevent those who are able from undertaking the valuable and ancient office of Church-warden: and that, whether in the Parish Vestries, or in the Meetings of our Rural Deaneries, or in the Diocesan Conferences, or as our representatives in the House of Laymen, Church Laymen will be ready to come forward and do their utmost to support that Church which is the indestructible and divinely appointed means of our salvation, and which has contributed so greatly to the Power and Peace of our Country.

I may, I feel sure, take this opportunity of offering on my own behalf, and on behalf of our whole Diocese, our grateful thanks to Sir Charles Anderson, Mr. A. S. Leslie Melville, the Right Hon. Edward Stanhope, and Sir William Welby-Gregory for their willingness to render such assistance in the House of Laymen.[2] It would be presumption to speak with confidence of

---

[2] The Honble. M. E. G. Finch-Hatton would have been nominated again for the House of Laymen, but he declined on account of the pressure of Parliamentary and other duties.

the great work which this newly-constituted assembly may accomplish; but all true Churchmen must be thankful that an attempt has been made by which the new problems of the Church's welfare may be discussed by the most competent persons, without violating the ancient Synodical Constitution of the Church.

2. *Our Schools.* To none perhaps should my thanks be more readily, or more sincerely, given than to the Inspectors of our Schools. I do desire to offer you my thanks most sincerely, on behalf of those whose Angels we know behold the Face of their Father in Heaven. Now, indeed, they do not themselves know what you have done for them, but they hereafter will be your joy and crown. It is indeed a most Christ-like and blessed work to see that children are taught the truths of Eternal Life.

Four hundred and fifty-two Schools have been visited by Diocesan Inspectors during the past year, a number which is again in excess of those inspected in any previous year; and the number would have been higher if all the reports had been sent in. More Schools are reported as good, fewer as fair, and still fewer as bad, than in any previous year. The numbers showing the degree of excellence of the Religious Instruction are—

	Schools.
Excellent or good in	338
Fair or moderate in	95
Indifferent or bad in	19
	452

No Church School has been given over to a Board during the year.

With regard to Pupil Teachers and Monitors, about the same number attended the Examination: but Canon Matthew doubts whether the results quite reached the usual level of excellence. When it can be done, I would earnestly remind my brethren of the Clergy, of the great importance of bringing the Pupil Teachers under their influence. They are the future Masters and Mistresses of our Schools; in moulding them we are moulding hundreds of our children. It is not merely by giving them definite instruction to help them in their different Examinations, valuable as that is, but by letting them know something of your mind and heart, that you will lift them up out of the low mechanical and mercantile view of their profession, and help them to realise, in some degree, the privilege of their high calling in training children, not only to be good citizens in this world, but of Heaven. I am glad to see by the answers to my Visitation Questions that many of the Clergy continue to give Religious Instruction in their Day Schools. I believe that the syllabus of religious instruction has wonderfully improved the religious teaching given by the Clergy in their Schools, by giving it method and precision. I wish I could feel quite as sure that there was the same hope and love centred in the Parish School as there was forty years ago.

There are still some Parishes insufficiently provided with Schools; and some Schools which are not under

Diocesan Inspection. I shall be glad, where this is the case, if the Clergy will communicate with me, that we may see if any remedy can be suggested.

The two difficulties which seem especially to demand our consideration are the early age at which our children leave our Country Schools (being generally in the Fourth Standard, and not older than 11), and the difficulty of maintaining an efficient Sunday School in Country Parishes, where the houses are scattered, where a Dissenting School may exist, and where few competent teachers are to be found.

The first difficulty is increased by the fact that Night-schools seem, speaking generally, to be no longer cared for; in a few instances they are still spoken of as doing well and flourishing, but the language of the returns generally is, " We used to have them, but they have ceased to attend ; the young men do not care to come ": the truth being that most of the young lads can read and write and do a little summing, and they care for nothing more.

I do not know what the complete answer to this difficulty ought to be, but let us remember that the difficulty is partly the result of success ; it is because we have quickly reached a certain point, which was not reached before, that there is, at present, no desire to learn more. Let this give us hope, and let us watch patiently and unweariedly till we see by what next step those who have thus risen may yet rise higher. There are some cases in country villages, and still more, of course, in towns, where the advantages of a prolonged education are easily shown by the possibility of obtaining places in offices, on the railway, or in domestic service. When this is the case, classes however small, however irregular, should be formed to give just that kind and degree of higher intellectual instruction which is found to be acceptable : but in the country villages there are many to whom this cannot apply.

Still let us not expect too much. It cannot be said of all the members of educated families that between the ages of eleven and twenty-two they have an intelligent interest in their own self-culture : the purely intellectual is not the ruling influence of their lives. Let the Parish be to us as our own family. Judging from the way in which we were educated ourselves, I cannot help suggesting that something more might be done in the direction of strengthening the religious principle, and in exercising, in innocent and intelligent amusement, the knowledge the young people have. With this object, I believe, in towns, clubs and reading-rooms, with lectures and music, and other innocent recreation, are found to answer ; and something of the same kind might be adapted, in winter months, to our villages. The village school, or a central club room, or a room in the vicarage, might be opened occasionally for a lecture, or a concert, or for classes in carving or art of some kind. Books and games, and papers and picture papers might be sent to the foremen at farm houses, or even to cottages, where possible. The moral value of games, as affording innocent occupation, *and subject for innocent conversation*,[3] is exceedingly great.

But with all this very *definite* and *persevering* efforts must also be made to deepen the religious principle. The failure of a beneficial influence in Athletics or Art has been due to the want of proportion in their use. When people have trusted to a philanthropic supply of amusements as a substitute for the Gospel, they have naturally been disappointed with the result. We want something in the poor lad's home which shall correspond to the patient, humble, wise, holy, and loving power which a mother's influence is in our own. Perhaps the wife and daughters at the Rectory, or the Hall, and the younger Clergy can best supply the need. Much, I know, they have already done.

We need some kindly light to lead the young people through the common age of wreckage, between the years of 17 and 27. The less-educated have hardly any adequate conception of the degree of self-mastery, self-culture, and self-sacrifice which a real life requires. This is to be gained by deepening the religious principle—by showing them the example of Christ, Who pleased not Himself; and teaching them that a Christ-like life may be (and should) be theirs.

This leads me to the second difficulty—the Sunday School. In towns there seems little in this matter to be desired, except that all should be encouraged to

[3] I am indebted for this thought to a Paper by the Head Master of Clifton College, Mr. Wilson.

persevere in their good work ; and where possible, that increasing opportunities should be devised for teaching the Teachers ; and perhaps a more graduated system of Catechising be adopted ; and more effective Children's Services. We should remember the rule of our Church in her Canon requiring all Fathers and Mothers, Masters and Mistresses to send not only the young, but the *ignorant* to be catechized ;—we should try to provide *Elementary Instruction* for the *adult ignorant* as well as for the young. The Sunday School in this sense might take the form of "*Instructions*" after Service on Sunday in the Church—and this during special seasons, as Advent and Lent. But in the country villages there is more need for anxiety.

The difficulties are, I know, almost insuperable— where the Clergyman is single-handed with, perhaps, two Churches ; where his people are scattered, and there are few to help. Still I will venture to ask :—

Are there not some cases where a Sunday School might be held where at present there is none ?

According to the *Diocesan Calendar* for 1886, 120 Parishes are without Sunday Schools. But by the Visitation Returns, 72 of these Parishes are re- turned as having Schools. Of the remaining 48—in 6 Parishes the children go elsewhere, 4 Parishes have made no return, and 6 Parishes have made uncertain returns. This will leave a remainder of 32 Parishes in which there does not appear to be any provision for a Sunday School.

Might we not find more Teachers if we took more
pains to explain to members of our own family, or
household, or to two or three more educated and pious
members of our congregation, what a proof of love to
our Blessed Lord it would be to feed His lambs?

Might we not in time create more Teachers of our
own, if we were content to work as our Divine Master
did, in a centrifugal manner, and so reach the many
through the few? A few children well taught, and
influenced by close and loving contact with the
Teacher's hand and heart, would themselves be
examples of what Christian children can be, and thus
unconscious teachers of others.

3. The religious teaching of the young leads me
naturally to speak of Confirmation. Here, my first
desire is to express to you the great satisfaction which
my Confirmation tour has given me, not only for the
good behaviour of the candidates, but for the evidence
of their religious capacity and interest. Most sincerely
do I, for His sake, thank you for your labour.

I have confirmed during the last eighteen months
5058 persons.[4] The number of candidates confirmed in
the Spring time is rather less than in the same district
two years ago. But there may have been sufficient causes
for this. Nevertheless this leads me to say, with a
sorrowful sincerity, that in some instances the number
of candidates presented was not I fear, judging from
the population, what it ought to have been. I can

[4] Autumn, 1885—Males. 742; Females, 1078. Spring, 1886—Males, 1327;
Females, 1746. Miscellaneous—Males, 73; Females, 92.

conceive, my brethren, few sorrows more bitter to the true Pastor's heart than to hear of someone who, through his negligence, had fallen from his first love— even though in God's mercy that negligence should be brought home to him by the cry of a returning penitent, "O God, unmake me, remake me, make me what I might have been if I had never sinned."

I am thankful to see by the returns to my questions that, on the whole, a satisfactory proportion of those confirmed have made their first Communion.

4. With regard to the frequency of Holy Communion I see from the Visitation Returns that the Parishes in which it is celebrated

Weekly, or more frequently, are 120.
Fortnightly... ... ... ,, 101.
Monthly .... ,, 288.
Less than Monthly ... ... ,, 86.

I have been glad to notice in several instances that the desire is expressed for more frequent Celebrations of the Holy Communion than it has been found possible at present to obtain. I should not desire to press any of my brethren forward in so sacred a matter with undue haste, but I earnestly hope that it will be the aim of all to celebrate the Holy Communion on all Sundays and Holy Days. In our smallest Country Parishes it may take some little time safely to reach this standard, but if it be accepted by all Incumbents, and made a definite part of their teaching in the Pulpit, and from house to house; and, moreover, if it be put before the people in the Parish as a great object for which they should work together, both by mutual arrangement between employed and employer, and also by the employed among themselves, then a very great improvement, I believe, might, by God's help, quickly be attained.

The proportion of newly Confirmed who make their *first* Communion fills one both with hope and anxiety. We must not expect too much from them, surrounded as they are by prejudices and temptations, but my belief is that a considerable number, if we could thoroughly win their confidence, would be both fit and glad to come more often afterwards than they do. There is room here for earnest prayer and watching. Communicant Classes, and Services for Preparation late on Friday or Saturday Evening, or before the first Sunday in the month, would often, I believe, be a help and comfort to many.

We must not expect too much from our people, or we shall dishearten them and ourselves too.

It would be better to try and find out just what standard we ought all reasonably to aim at now, things being as they are, and then to see what higher standard we should be justified in working towards, not aiming necessarily at a uniformity, much less at a simultaneous uniformity, of practice, but waiting upon God's Will.

Thus though we have, no doubt, fallen below the Scriptural and Primitive Standard and the Standard of our own Church, which requires every Parishioner to communicate three times a year, yet I believe we may be thankful for the position which our Communicants hold, in the present state of Christendom.

The standard, with regard to frequency of Communion, from Scripture and the Early Church, given in Bingham (*Eccl. Antiq.*, Bk. xv., chp. 18), shows the following results :—

1. *Weekly.*

" It is certain," he says, " it was both the rule and practice for all in general, both clergy and laity, to receive the Communion every Lord's Day, except Catechumens or Penitents." The Scriptural Evidence is Acts xx. 7, " and upon the first day of the week, when the disciples came together to break bread."

The Patristic evidence is explicit in Justin Martyr Apol. ii , A.D. 140, and in the writings of many others.

2. *Three or Four times a week.*

" It appears undeniable that in many Churches they had the Communion four times every week, on Wednesdays, Fridays, Saturdays and Sundays, besides incidental festivals, which were very frequent."

3. *Daily.*

" In some places they received the Communion every day "; and again —" In the greater Churches, probably, they had it every day ; in the lesser only once or twice a week."

S. Cyprian (*de Orat. Dom.*) and others speak of th Holy Eucharist as the Daily Bread.

S. Augustine (*Ep.* liv. *ad Januar :*) states the practice, in his time, most fully.

"Alii quotidie communicant Corpori ac Sanguini Domini, alii certis diebus accipiunt : alibi nullus dies praetermittitur, quo non offeratur, alibi sabbato tantum et Dominica, alibi tantum Dominica ; et si quid aliud hujusmodi animadverti potest, totum hoc genus rerum liberas habet observationes": and later in the Ep. S. Augustine compares these who desire to receive daily, and those who desire to receive less frequently, to Zacchæus and the Centurion. ' Nam et ille honorando non audet quotidie sumere, et ille honorando non audet ullo die praetermittere."

While there is abundant Patristic authority for Daily Communion in some places, I cannot think that the Catechism of the Council of Trent is justified in saying that Daily Communion is the norma certissima of S. Augustine, as if it were the uniform standard to aim at, or that this was the opinion of all the Fathers. " Eundem sensum fuisse omnium Patrum."*

The present Roman rule requiring all to communicate *once* a year is late, dating from the Council of Lateran, A.D. 1216. The rule of our own Rubric requiring *three* times a year is older, as old as the Council of Agde, A.D. 506.

But the practice of the earliest centuries was more scriptural when both clergy and laity received the Holy Communion every Sunday at least.

Let it then be the aim in every Parish, both of priest and people, an aim for which they will work and pray

---

* The sermon of S. Augustine, from which the Catechism quotes, is Sermon 84 in the Appendix, which, however, some ascribe to S. Ambrose.

together, that the Holy Communion should be celebrated every Sunday. If priest and people were really to make this a great object of their lives, there would be few, if any, parishes without a weekly Eucharist. And here I must quote one of the (for us) most sad regulations on this great subject; it is the Resolution of the Plan of Pacification put forth by the Wesleyan body shortly after John Wesley's death. During John Wesley's lifetime, it is well known, the Holy Communion was never administered in their chapels by their ministers, but four years after his death the following resolution was adopted.

" We agree that the Lord's Supper be administered amongst us on Sundays . . . . . nevertheless it shall never be administered on those Sundays on which it is administered in the Parochial Church."—Peirce's *Wesleyan Polity*, p. 139.

5. The condition of our Parish Churches, thanks to the energy of my three immediate Predecessors, and the liberality of the Clergy and Laity alike, shows a very marked improvement on what it must have been at the beginning of the Century.

During the past eighteen months I have consecrated 5 Churches. Our greatest difficulties perhaps now arise from *inconvenience of position*, when the Church is far away from the village, or the population is completely scattered, and from *cold*. The expense of warming is, I know, a great difficulty, but, as far as it is possible, I feel convinced that it is of the utmost importance to make our Churches *comfortable*, and comfortable *for poor and rich alike*. It is not, I believe, so much the *simplicity* of the Dissenting Chapel which attracts, as its nearness and its *warmth*. Few acts of charity would, I believe, be more richly blessed than for the rich, when the cold weather begins, to look round and see that the Churches in their own neighbourhoods are, at least on Sundays, made thoroughly warm.

There is, however, still building and restoration for us to do. 157 Churches are returned as needing restoration of one kind or another : and in our large towns, especially in Grimsby, new Churches are needed. I trust those to whom God has given the means will consider our needs and help me in this great work for God.[5]

With regard to the Church-yards I find from the returns that burials with services conducted by Ministers not of the Church of England have taken place in 58 Parishes or Cemeteries. As this is, I am thankful to say, so small a proportion of the whole number of our Parishes, nearly 600, I see no reason to go back from the announcement that I made of my readiness to consecrate the burial grounds wherever it is desired.[6]

6. The non-residence of the Clergy is, I hope, except in some sad cases, nearly confined to those who

[5] The rapid growth of the town of Grimsby has made its spiritual needs very great. The population has reached 50,000 ; and I am told the number of houses built there during the past year equals the number built in the whole of the rest of the County. It is of the greatest importance that we should lose no time in providing Church privileges for the people.

[6] These returns refer in several cases to single burials, and apparently extend over the whole period since the passing of the Act of 1880.

are absent from the necessities of their health, or the health of their families.

The increase of Parsonage Houses has no doubt largely contributed to the residence of the Clergy, and to the great social blessing which all acknowledge the presence of the Clergyman and his family to be, as a link between the different classes in the land. The chief ground for anxiety with regard to such houses would seem to be that they should be kept in fitting proportion with the income of the living, and in position should be accessible to the people, and convenient for frequent attendance in the Church. The desire during the last 50 years to obtain residences for the Clergy has led, in some instances, to the invitation of men of wealth to build houses which are out of proportion with the means of the Parish.

I desire to commend again to your prayers and to your liberal support the various Institutions which the wisdom and liberality of my predecessors, and others, have founded in our Diocese. Among them I would mention—

(a) *The Bishop's Hostel,* Bishop Wordsworth's College at Lincoln. My sincere thanks are due to the Chancellor, the Rev. Canon Leeke; and to the Rev. Canon Crowfoot and the Rev. E. H. R. Tatham, and the other members of the tutorial staff, for the untiring zeal and ability with which they have continued their labours.

The question of training Candidates for Holy Orders is one to which I have been permitted to give by far the greater part of my ministerial life, more than a quarter-of-a-century : but it is too great and too important to be considered in a mere passing notice ; enough for the present that I offer you the Chancellor's report on the present condition of our College, and commend it again to your sympathy and your prayers.[7]

Since the opening of the College in 1874, there have been 278 Students, of whom 54 had a University Degree. There are in residence this Term *48 Students, of whom 10 are Graduates. During the past year 14 Students of the College have been admitted to the Diaconate, and 13 to the Priesthood, of whom 6 Deacons and 8 Priests are working in the Diocese.[8]

(b) *Our Mission College at Burgh.* For this I will more definitely ask your assistance. I desire to offer

[7] I have Ordained 23 Priests, and 32 Deacons ; of the Deacons 14 were Graduates, 18 Non-Graduates.

May I take this opportunity of reminding my brethren to press upon their people the duty of observing the Ember Seasons, as the Prayer Book directs, with special prayer and fasting.

* This number is exceptionally large, owing to the fact that several Students are remaining with us after the completion of their course.

[8] The period of residence is 2 years (6 terms) for non-Graduates ; for Graduates one year or less, by arrangement.

The expenses to each Student may be estimated at £80 a year, exclusive of Vacations. In reduction of these 4 Bursaries are offered each year of the value of £40 each for 2 years, so that 8 Students are at any one time in receipt of a Bursary.

The Bishop's Hostel pays its way and enables us to set aside more than £100 a year in reduction of the original debt on the Furnishing Fund. The rent of Lindum Holme, together with the Student's Tuition Fees (£30 a year each) forms a Fund out of which we are at present able to pay £805 to our Tutorial Staff, and £320 to the maintenance of 8 Bursaries. It will be seen that, as there are 6 Members of the Tutorial Staff, this arrangement can only be carried on by the generous co-operation of those concerned.

my grateful thanks to the Rev. W. A. Brameld for the untiring patience and self-sacrificing zeal with which he continues to win, and mould, and fit for still higher training, the students committed to his care. The condition of our College is most encouraging. It is quite full; the Committee report as follows :—(and here let me offer them and especially the Rev. S. Staffurth, Honorary Secretary, and W. Lane-Claypon, Esq., my sincere thanks for their freely given labours) "Every year the Mission House proves more and more its *raison d' être;* every year it gains in standing, and in its just demands upon the confidence and support of the Diocese."

The Principal's own report tells us—"The work of the Mission House, both spiritual and intellectual, has, I trust, been going on as satisfactorily as we could expect, and I am thankful to be able to note that a higher level seems, in some measure at any rate, to be attained in both respects. The reports of the Examiners speak of an advance intellectually in the House, while there is every reason to be thankful and hopeful as to the spiritual standard aimed at by the whole body of Students."

The College has been enlarged by the addition of a new wing, called, after the generous benefactor by whom it has been built, "The Wordsworth Wing."

All this is well : but the Committee report a falling off in the annual subscriptions and offertories ; in 1878 they amounted to £269 17s. ; in 1886 they are only £170 17s. 5d. : nearly £100 less. This has been no doubt chiefly through the death and removal of former friends, but it should arrest our attention, and will, I trust, quicken your sympathy. The sum required is not large, about £30 a year more are needed for the Bursary Fund, to place it in a satisfactory condition. If those who are especially able would communicate with the Secretary or Treasurer, they would learn what sum is required. I believe there are many who will be willing to avail themselves of the privilege of giving and collecting money to train those who are to spread the Gospel in Heathen Lands.[9] In thus pressing upon your consideration the needs of our Diocesan Missionary College, I would not have you forget the great Parent Missionary Societies—the Society for the Propagation of the Gospel and Church Missionary Society.

. (c) *Novate Novale, or the Society of Mission Clergy.*—This Society had its origin in a letter written by Chancellor Benson in the month of September, 1875.

At the close of a decade we ask: How far have our hopes been realized? Has the Society fulfilled the promise of its beginning?

[9] I cannot refrain from printing the words which have reached me a few days ago from a distinguished Missionary in Zanzibar (A. C. Madan, Esq.) The words, Mr. Madan says, are from a letter written to him by a native boy, teaching what he had learnt, as well as he could, to other black boys, in an island of Lake Nyassa. "Ring the bell in England, Sir, and tell the great men of the Universities to send us white teachers, for there are many here who have never seen a white man, or heard of God. Tell them not to lose a minute." It is a grateful pleasure to me to be able to let this young Christian's words be heard in this Diocese. May God bless them according to His will!

1. This Society was, I believe, the first Diocesan Society organized to promote the holding of Parochial Missions. It has thus been the forerunner of several societies which have been formed during the last ten years. Similar organizations, all drawn up more less closely after the model of its rule, now exist in the Dioceses of Bath and Wells, Gloucester and Bristol, Norwich, Peterborough, and Salisbury. Yet more close, in all probability, is the relation in which it stands to the office of Canon Missioner in the Diocese of Truro, and, through the Diocese of Truro, to the similar offices which have been called into being in the Dioceses of Lichfield, Durham, and, more recently, of Canterbury.

2. Bishop Wordsworth was a true prophet when he sketched the character of the Country Parson as a Missioner. His picture has become a living reality. The best Missioners of the Society have been the Pastors of Country Parishes, and in some instances of very small parishes indeed. Men of study, and meditation and prayer, they have gone forth like the eremites of old, and year by year have conducted Missions in this and other Dioceses. It would be faithless to doubt, and unthankful to the Giver of all Grace, not to acknowledge the blessings which we know to have followed their teaching and preaching. It would, however, be well to look round, and see by what methods this our Society of Mission Clergy may be made more of a Diocesan Agency. Its original purpose was for the benefit of the Diocese, at least in

the first instance, and I will ask all who are interested in its welfare to consider in what ways we might increase its Diocesan efficiency. I shall be glad to receive suggestions from any of the Clergy or Laity on this point.

(*d*) *Augmentation of Small Benefices.*—How greatly this valuable Association is needed may be gathered from the appeal printed in the Report; in which it is stated that of the 588 Benefices in Lincolnshire, the income of one-ninth is not more than £100 a year; the income of one-third does not exceed £200 a year; and of half is not more than £300 : indeed, there are few matters more worthy of our serious and united consideration than the maintenance and increase of the funds for providing spiritual aid in our Diocese. How highly my benevolent predecessor valued this Society he showed to the last by bequeathing a legacy of £500 to its funds. I earnestly commend this good work to the sympathy of all, reminding you that "a number of small contributions, making up together £100 towards the augmentation of any small Benefice, will as fully effect that purpose as the gift of the whole sum by one person."

(*e*) *A Fund for the Relief of certain necessitous Clergymen and Widows and Orphans of Clergymen.*

Our grateful thanks are due to the Rev. Canon Smyth and others, for their labours in support of this fund. In the present agricultural distress few funds are more worthy of support. If means could be obtained to provide assistance for aged or infirm

Incumbents, it would relieve the smaller livings of the burden of a retiring pension, which too often results in the crippling poverty of both the old and new Incumbent.

(*f*) *The Training College for Mistresses in our Schools.* This excellent Institution continues under the wise and loving experience of Canon Nelson to maintain its usual efficiency. To him, and to those who work with him, we owe our continued thanks.

From the printed Report of last year I gather that the supply of Candidates was almost the same as the year before, 98 against 99. Of these, in Religious Knowledge, 5 obtained a place in the First Class, 30 were in the Second, 49 in the Third, and 15 failed. In Secular Knowledge 12 were placed in the First Class, 51 in the Second, 9 in the Third, and 27 failed.

The same Report tells us that the health of the Students "has been very good." "The financial position of the Training College continues to be highly satisfactory."

Canon Nelson tells me in a private letter this year, "the finance, health, and all essentials continue in as satisfactory a state as when the Report of last year was printed." I have only to remind you that this year Canon Nelson will have carried on his excellent work for a quarter of a century. Many will, I am sure, be glad that I should assure him of their gratitude, their sympathy, and their prayers.

(*g*) *The Hospital, Lincoln.*—This ancient and excellent Institution, under the Presidency of Earl

Brownlow, continues to carry on its benevolent work with thorough efficiency. "The Medical Officers express themselves quite satisfied with the general condition of the Hospital, and consider the Nursing to be efficiently performed." I am sorry, however, to learn from the Yearly Report[1] that there is again a falling off in the Subscriptions : so that in spite of the strictest economy, "scarcely a week passes but patients are refused admission an account of want of accommodation." I desire to commend this truly Christian Institution to your renewed and increased support.

(*h*) *Mablethorpe Convalescent Home.*—All who have had the privilege of visiting the poor in their homes must be well wishers to this kindly and hopeful Institution. Too often the good received in the Hospital is lost by the necessity of returning at once to work, or to a noisy and comfortless home. Mablethorpe is not a Hospital, but a Home, where rest, and brightness, and fresh air, and sea bathing, may, by God's blessing, make the convalescent strong. The buildings have been enlarged, and now leave little or nothing to be desired. There is accommodation for 61 Patients. The cost of enlargement has been £1100, and though the Subscriptions have been, we are thankful to say, well maintained, there is need of additional donations to furnish the new apartments. For this work especially I ask your assistance, and desire to commend again our Institution to your sympathy and aid.

[1] Cf. 116th Annual Report, 1885.

(*i*) *The Lincoln Institution for Nurses.*—The 19th Report of this most useful Institution tells us that "the work has been carried on as usual, and presents no feature calling for special comment."

I cannot, however, commend this good work again to your sympathy without expressing the great loss which the Institution has sustained since the Report was printed, in the death of Mrs. Bromhead. To her wise and kind superintendence the Institution is greatly indebted for its present efficiency. The Nurses, and many of the sick, will, I feel sure, unite with me in offering this grateful tribute to her memory.

There are now 47 fully trained Nurses employed. Two, and often more Nurses regularly attend, *gratis*, cases of illness among the poor; 148 such cases have been attended during the present year in Lincoln and its neighbourhood. To continue this charitable part of our work, and to maintain so excellent an Institution generally, I thankfully and confidently ask the continuance of your support.

(*j*) *Church of England Temperance Society.*— The public service rendered by the Temperance movement has been acknowledged by our Judges, and by many public men who do not themselves belong to any Temperance Society.

The evil of drink was so strong and so widely spread, that it needed organization and public protest to check it.

The Lincolnshire Church of England Temperance Society has lately been newly organized, the Diocese being divided into eleven Districts, with Honorary District Secretaries, and with an Honorary Diocesan Secretary for the general work. To them, as well as to other kind friends and helpers, our sincere thanks are due.

The value of the Temperance movement is not confined to reclaiming the drunkard, glorious as such a work is. Temperance in drink is an easily understood example of that self-respect, self-control, self-mastery, which every man must attain if he would be the true man God intended him to be.

I cannot help therefore asking my brethren of the Clergy whether they have sufficiently considered the advantages which the Church of England Temperance Society might bring to their Parishes?

I observe by the Report that there are but 79 Parochial Branches in the 588 Benefices in the Diocese; and 25 of these are in the large towns: 8 are in Grimsby.

Are not the words of the Report very true? "It may be difficult, or even impossible, to carry on a Temperance Society in some Parishes, but are there many Parishes where a Temperance Meeting may not occasionally be held with advantage?"

With a view to bringing the value of the principles of this Society more generally before the people, I propose to ask the Clergy of this Diocese on the Third Sunday in Lent to preach Special Sermons on its behalf.

There are still, alas! thousands every year who are ruined by this sin; and tens of thousands in whom the spiritual sight is made dim, and whose usefulness and happiness are needlessly wasted.

(*k*) *Other good work in the Diocese.*—Besides these more formally Diocesan Societies there are, thank God, many other valuable, benevolent, and Christian agencies at work amongst us; such as the Girls' Friendly Society, the Young Women's Help Society, the Church of England Working Men's Society—all, and each of them, I desire to commend to your consideration and support, believing that, by God's blessing, they may be the means of drawing us nearer to one another, and to Himself.

8. Three new efforts have been made this year to meet the moral and spiritual needs of the Diocese.

One is the carrying into effect a Resolution of a Committee of the Diocesan Conference of 1883, for the Establishment of a Penitentiary.

This merciful work has been happily commenced at Frieston, near Boston; 11 Penitents are already in the House, under the charge of three Sisters from Horbury. The Rev. S. Staffurth, Vicar of the Parish, most kindly gives his services as Chaplain, and W. Lane-Claypon, Esq., has most disinterestedly consented to act as Treasurer. To them both, and to the whole Committee, I offer my grateful thanks. We hope to earn as much as possible by washing sent from Boston; but still the Institution will require the charitable support of friends; about £230 a year are equired. To meet this we have at present Subscriptions, £120; Offertories, £50; and £50 we have applied for current expenses from the Donation Fund, which ought to be left as a beginning of a fund for the ultimate purchase of the House : there is, therefore, immediate need of an increase of annual subscriptions to the amount of £60. I hope that this Institution may form part of a more complete scheme for carrying on this much needed work in the Diocese, by the establishment of Houses, or Refuges, in our towns, and by establishing Branches of the Church of England Purity Society, not only in our towns, but in our country villages. No one with a true Christian heart can be content to rest and leave things as they are, and to see the bloom and fruit of our youth, year after year, marred by needless sin from which they might have been saved. I earnestly hope that many will be glad of this opportunity of rescuing the fallen, and of giving a contribution to the evidences of the Christian faith by joining in this Christlike work, and vindicating the power of the Grace of Christ. It is for His glory—they are members of His Body, for whom we ask your aid —and they should be as Jewels in His Crown.

The Rev. S. Staffurth or Mr. W. L. Claypon will, I am sure, be ready to give any information that may be required, and supply Boxes and Cards for the collection of small sums.

A second effort is the Society for raising money in aid of Additional Curates. It has been found in other Dioceses that a Ladies' Association for this purpose has met with marked success ; and all will, I am sure, join with me in expressing our grateful thanks to Miss

Susan Wordsworth for giving us the assistance of her labour, and the influence of her name, to further so good a cause. So far the effort has been well responded to. The Association has already begun its work in twenty out of the forty Rural Deaneries in the Diocese, and upwards of £60 has already been subscribed. Working parties have been formed both in the towns and in country villages, and have been well attended; and it is hoped that before the end of another year the Association will be represented throughout the Diocese. I desire to commend the effort to your continued sympathy and support.

The third effort that has been made is in accordance with a resolution passed at the Diocesan Conference last year, when it was resolved that a Diocesan Magazine should be started, as in Lichfield, and some other Dioceses. By the aid of the Committee, and by the intelligent zeal of the Rev. R. E. Warner, who has most kindly undertaken the responsible and laborious office of Editor, this has been done; and, so far, the effort bids fair to succeed. Between one thousand and fifteen hundred copies have been circulated, and many subscribers have expressed themselves with satisfaction and pleasure for the information they have received. I offer my sincere thanks to the Committee, and especially to the Editor, and to all our kind friends who have helped us by their contributions. I trust that our Magazine may, under God's blessing, be a bond of union amongst us, reminding us of our common work, and making us, more and more, of one mind and of one heart in our Master's service.

Before I close this portion of my charge I desire to make one suggestion, on which I shall be glad to have your opinion and counsel, and the resolutions of your Chapters in the Rural Deaneries. Now that the Diocese is limited to one County, we have special opportunities for renewed unity of Diocesan action. There is, I believe, room for an increase of such unity. The Diocese, though now limited to one County, is still more or less divided by the threefold divisions of the County. I am, therefore, anxious to learn whether you would think it advisable that we should establish a Board, composed of Clergy and Laity together, for three principal Diocesan Societies for *Spiritual Aid, Church Building (with Parsonage Houses),* and *Education.* Such a Board, gathered from all parts of the Diocese, and meeting once a quarter in Lincoln, would bring before us, for common discussion, the various local needs in different parts of the County, which without some such general organization may be over-looked, or be unable to obtain sufficient assistance in the separated districts. I feel sure that such a Board would be of very great assistance to myself, in enabling me to know what the great needs of the Diocese are, and, as far as possible, in helping me to devise means to relieve them. There need be no immediate hurry in the establishment of such a Board; but I shall be grateful for your consideration of this scheme, and it might be further discussed, please God, next year at the Diocesan Conference.

If this suggestion should be carried into effect, I

should propose to issue a Pastoral Letter each year on behalf of one of the three Societies.

SUMMARY AND CONCLUSION.

From these particular needs of our Diocese, let me now in conclusion pass to some general reflexions suggested by the answers to my Visitation questions. But first let me thank you for the trouble you have taken to give me the information I desired.

If I were only to use the language of praise, such praise would be valueless. Bear with me then, my brethren, if I say that there are some Parishes in our Diocese which cause me much anxiety, and in which I fear there must be a sad forgetfulness of the solemn words of the Ordination Service. "Have always, therefore, printed in your remembrance how great a treasure is committed to your charge. For they are the sheep of Christ, which he bought with His death, and for whom He shed His blood. The Church and Congregation whom you must serve, is His Spouse, and His Body ; and if it shall happen the same Church, or any member thereof, to take any hurt or hindrance by reason of your negligence, ye know the greatness of the fault, and also the horrible punishment that will ensue."

There are Parishes where there seems to be little or no provision made for the religious instruction of the young, from which few or no Candidates were presented for Confirmation, or where, of such Candidates as were presented, few, or none, made their first Communion ;

where the Holy Communion is but rarely celebrated, and where, though the population is not large, the Communicants do not number more than one-fortieth, or one-sixtieth, or even one-hundredth part of the people: while in other Parishes of the same size, or larger, the proportion of Communicants is one-tenth, or one-fifth, or one-third. Brethren, these are the places where Church Reform is most needed, and where it may most safely begin. They are "spots" and "blemishes," and grievous causes of offence ; not only in the Parishes where the wrong is done, but to the whole neighbourhood. The weeds that spring up in the field that is uncultivated scatter their seeds beyond the limits of the neglected land.

It will be my duty, after due warning, and with all fatherly forbearance and gentleness, to use such power as the Law may give me to redress these wrongs. The recent additions to the Pluralities Act were made for this purpose.

Brethren, I do not *judge*, I do not know either the special difficulties which may exist in these Parishes, or the unavailing efforts which may have been made to meet them. There is One Who knows all things ; but my duty is, for my own sake, and for your sake, and for the Flock, to *warn* and remind you of the word which came to the Prophet of old. "If the watchman see the sword come, and blow not the trumpet; if the sword come, and take any person from among them, he is taken away in his iniquity ; but his blood will I require at the watchman's hand."— *Ezekiel xxxiii.*, 6.

This short word of warning, my brethren, I have given you as a proof of my sincerity. Pardon it, if it is undeserved ; accept it, if it be in accordance with His will.

But do not let me be misunderstood; even in these words of warning there is ground for hope. The wrongs which call forth this warning are not such wrongs as in former years were known as " Clerical Scandals ": there is no insinuation implied of any breach of social morality. The wrong refers rather to ministerial neglect, or incapacity. The improved moral tone among the Laity has relieved the Clergy of many of the duties which formerly they rendered to the County as Magistrates, and Guardians, and upholders of Law and Order in their several neighbourhoods. The increased interest in Church affairs shown by many of the Laity leads them to desire a higher standard of ministerial efficiency in their Clergy. It is want of zeal, want of Scriptural and theological knowledge, want of spiritual capacity to undertake the " cure and government " of souls, which now forms the ground of complaint, and raises the cry of Reform. It is not simply a higher moral tone, but more ministerial efficiency which is required.

From this short word of *warning*, which an honest consideration of the answers which I have received seemed to require, I gladly pass to a final word of direct *encouragement*. Indeed this is the general impression left on my mind after considering the returns from the Diocese—the need of encouragement. I would that I knew how to give it effectually : but it is *something* when our trouble is noticed and recognised. In many parts of the Diocese there seems to be a sense of depression, a loss of brightness, a want of hope— and this, I think, from four principal causes.

1. *The decrease of Income.*—This is an almost universal complaint, and the cause often of the greatest anxiety, and, I fear, in some cases of great distress. Where there is a family to educate, or where there is sickness, it often must be so. If the price of corn remains as it is, it is difficult to see the remedy. Something might be done to bring the incomes of the Clergy more on an equality ; but in the present uncertain value of land it is important that any charge made upon the richer Livings to relieve the poorer, should not be a fixed sum, but a proportion of the net annual income of the Living upon which the charge is made ; and that the sum charged should bear its proportion of the rates and taxes. Greater facilities might be given for holding two, or more, small livings together, either by consolidation or in plurality. Two causes seem to point to this—the decrease of income, and the increase of zeal and devotion among the younger Clergy. They will not accept livings where there is little to do. It may seem a retrograde movement to give up the residence of the Parish Priest in each Parish ; but apart from the almost necessity of the case, I believe the increased ministerial zeal and efficiency might more than compensate for the loss. As the work of a Priest is better understood, both by Priest and people alike,

it will be possible to use more freely the assistance of duly authorised Laymen, and thus to commit a larger area, with a larger income, to the care of individual Priests. The difficulty lies chiefly with the Patrons.

But meanwhile the anxiety and distress go on : and I can only appeal on behalf of my brethren to any to to whom God may have given the means, to consider in what way they may relieve the anxiety of their poorer brethren ; especially, if I may suggest one way out of many, by helping them to carry out the education of their sons at the Universities, in order. that they may be ordained. I fear one of the greatest evils of the present clerical distress will be the loss to the Church in the future of just those very persons, who, by social position, and inherited culture, and early training in their fathers' Parishes, would, with the addition of a University education, be the fittest candidates for Holy Orders—I mean the sons of our present Clergy. The depression and distress are so much the greater because they have come upon us unexpectedly. Husbands cannot make the homes they had reason to expect for their families. I do not believe that poverty would intimidate men from offering themselves for the Ministry, much less that it could destroy the Church of England ; only let men know what to expect, and what is expected of them ; let their spiritual position be clearly understood, let them have free access to the people, and if it be God's will to take away our income I believe it may go without loss of happiness or spiritual power. But, as it is, there is distress. "Blessed is the man that considereth the poor and needy."

2. *Dissent.*—A second cause of depression is the prevalence of Dissent. The influence of Dissent is depressing in many ways: it divides the congregation, it weakens the school, it makes it more difficult to keep up a choir, it interferes with the discipline of the Parish, it destroys the feeling of confidence which unity gives, it turns the cords by which we would draw our people into a rope of sand, it substitutes a spirit of disintegrating individualism for the bond of Church principles.

This is true, and is hard to bear, especially in small Parishes; but we ought not to be too much depressed, and it should be a matter of faith not to lose heart. A very small portion of our Dissent is Theologically hostile to the Church. Those who go to Chapel go to Church too. Of all the answers to my Visitation Questions there is *only one instance* in which definite unbelief is mentioned. In the main our people are believers in God, and in our Lord Jesus Christ; they are baptized, they hold to the Bible, they are frequent in prayer and praise. Truly in all this there is matter for great thankfulness and hope. With some sad exceptions, which speak of half the population going nowhere; or, even worse, where the language is, "as a rule the agricultural labourer seems to go nowhere;" with these sad exceptions, I do not gather from the Visitation Returns that actual godlessness is so prevalent amongst us as I have sometimes feared. I have been thankful to see that the large majority are seeking to worship God and our Saviour Jesus Christ. There is, I believe, among our people an imperfect, but a very real and precious, belief in and love of God. Nevertheless we should take pains to let our Nonconformist brothers clearly understand what we mean. We should tell them that by virtue of their Baptism they have been made members of the Catholic Church, that they have been incorporated into the Body of Christ; but that in failing to continue stedfast in the Apostles' doctrine and fellowship, and in the Breaking of Bread and in the Prayers, and by setting up rival places of worship they are, so far, separating themselves from the covenanted sacramental means of grace. We must tell them plainly that though they are members of Christ's Body the Church, they are so in virtue of their Baptism and in spite of the distinctive tenets of the different sects, which tend to draw them away from the Unity of the Faith. We must remember Hezekiah's prayer, "the good Lord pardon every one that prepareth his heart to seek God, the Lord God of his fathers, though he be not cleansed according to the purification of the sanctuary." [2]

We in Lincolnshire have the birth-place of John Wesley: and it should be our unceasing prayer and effort to be among the first to bring back his followers to the church to which he belonged, and which he exhorted them never to leave. "Be Church of England men still," are John Wesley's own words.

[2] II. Chron. xxx. 18, 19.

I will not repeat what I have said already, as to
the true way in which, I believe, this may be done ;
viz., by the faithful and loving inculcation of Church
Doctrine as being indeed Bible Truth :[3] but I will ask
you once more to listen to the words of my great predecessor, Bishop Wordsworth: "Wesleyanism, he says,"
" is to be ascribed to our non-inculcation of the dis-"
" tinctive doctrines of the Church, and to our non-"
" observance of her laws.   Clerical non-residence,"
" churches closed from Sunday to Sunday, single "
" services on Sundays,—sometimes only once a fort-"
" night—cold, dry, dreary essays read from the "
" pulpit, instead of heart-stirring sermons preached ;"
" infrequent Communions, neglect of the sacred "
" seasons, the Fasts and Festivals of the Church,"
" monotonous music drawling on in dirge-like strains,"
" instead of a living flood of melody gushing forth in "
" full streams from the hearts and lips of the whole "
" Congregation of Worshippers—these were the causes "
" of Wesleyanism. . . . 'For my own part, the "
" great Bishop adds,' 'I feel a strong persuasion that "
" our best method of healing this unhappy breach is "
" to make the Church of England to be in practice "
" what she is in theory."[4]
It is brethren, because I believe that this is just what
is going on amongst us increasingly, that I bid you
not to lose heart. Our ground of confidence is that
we are sowing good seed. Enough for the Disciple

[3] See Prebendary Sadler's excellent little book with that title.
[4] Primary Charge, 1870, pp. 76, 77.

that he be as his Master, Who came not as a reaper but was content as a *Sower* to go forth to sow.

3. A third constant cause of discouragement is the annual change of the greater part of at least the younger portion of our people. No sooner are they prepared for Confirmation than they leave ; and happy is it both for Priest and people if they have made their first Communion ; still it is disheartening year after year to begin again with new faces and with the feeling that they " will also go away."

What can I say to this ? I think, Brethren, we may derive some relief if we can make it the opportunity for rising out of one of the dangers of our Parochial system, Ministerial jealousy.

Pardon me if I seem hard, but there is danger in the Parochial system of a certain narrowness of soul which makes us forget that there is really but One Shepherd, and *one Flock*, and that we are but Shepherds under Him. The intensity of pure love which is required to be concentrated on each soul to convince it of its capacity to receive the love of God, makes the exercise of the spirit of detachment and self-sacrifice implied in a continually changing flock, exceedingly hard : only by the grace of God can it be attained ; but to God all things are possible. For ourselves a heart more completely given to Christ would be the remedy. A more spiritual insight into the reality of the union between Christ and His Flock, to see Him in them, and them in Him, would make us ready to welcome each of the new comers as they came, and to find our satisfaction and rest not in uniting them to ourselves, but to Him. And for the young people themselves, when they leave us might we not find help by establishing for them a Guild or Society, by whatever name it may be called, which should be wider than the narrow limits of the Parish, and yet by its definite, but simple rules touch them more closely than the great brotherhood of the Catholic Church? The advantages of such religious societies are generally two-fold, they are the shield of love, the safeguard against solitude on the one hand, and on the other, by their wise and simple regulations, they are the safeguard against religious extravagance and eccentricity.

The Wesleyan District Register is an instance of the value of such a method. Might we not establish a Diocesan Society both for young men and young women which would explain at once to the Clergy their religious position as they passed from one Parish to another, and be to the young people themselves as a continuous voice of warning and encouragement in the first weeks of their loneliness in their new homes?

I shall be very glad, if such a scheme is considered possible, to call together a Committee to carry it into effect. Loneliness, solitude, is a great hindrance to perseverance in excellence of any kind, and the frequent cause of sin.

4. The fourth and last cause of discouragement which I have noted is the smallness of many of the Parishes. The difficulty of obtaining any kind of practical organization in such a Parish is very real. The Day-

School, the Choir, the Night School, can hardly be maintained. Confirmation and Communicant Classes must be small. The Sunday Congregation the same. Week-day congregations almost impossible. In a Parish of two or three thousand there are always some cases of special interest : in populations of one or two hundred it is not so. They do exist, and are of equal interest and importance, but they occur but rarely, there are dull monotonous intervals with little to excite. To preach to a crowded Church with a congregation of 800 or 1000 souls is itself stimulating, but to preach in a Church three parts full to a congregation of 60 or 30, Sunday after Sunday. requires a purer zeal. There are few or no secondary causes of assistance.

What can we say to this? First, I would remind you. my dear Brethren, of our Divine Master's example. When He came down to this earth, He did not come to the great cities of Greece or Italy, but confined His ministry to a relatively obscure portion of the world; and even in the narrow limits of Palestine He did not confine His teaching to the towns, but went through the cities *and villages* teaching, journeying towards Jerusalem. Indeed, this seems to me, to be the very picture that we need: teaching in the villages, but continually drawing nearer to our heavenly home, making progress in our own Spiritual Life. He taught in the villages, *journeying towards Jerusalem*, and Jerusalem meant for Him Calvary, and the Ascension and return to the Father.

It is encouraging to see that our small Parishes give us the most satisfactory results of Parochial

Work; the highest averages of Confirmation Candidates and Communicants are to be found there. It is most encouraging: for it shows that where the ministrations of the Church are more brought home to the people she is the more accepted. Our small Parishes should be to the rest of the Diocese as the seed plots which gardeners keep in their gardens, from which they plant out the plants they have there raised. We need some patterns, some models, of what English Agricultural poor can be, when they have been made intelligent members of the Church. We do not know yet what spiritual capacity and beauty there is in our people; from our acceptance of the low average standard which we have inherited from past neglect. Our Blessed Lord worked in a centrifugal way; radiating from Himself knowledge and holiness, reaching the many, through the few. His method of training was first by giving men Companionship with Himself, and then by sending them away to teach. "He ordained twelve *that they should be with Him, and that He might send them forth to preach.*" [5]

He sat alone at the well and gave his time to one; and she a schismatic and socially fallen. But His treatment was *thorough*, both *morally*, "he whom thou now hast is not thy husband," and *doctrinally*, "I that speak unto thee am He." And she became a believer herself, and an apostle to others. Would not a greater thoroughness in individual teaching go far to relieve the dullness of our Country Parishes? Other con-

[5] S. Mark. iii. 14.

siderations also might be always present to the Priest of the smallest Parish. The young people will be sure to change and go to other parts of the Diocese—any of my people or their children may emigrate to foreign lands. Will they carry good seed with them to sow in the new country, or, from my neglected field, shall I scatter, I know not whither, the tares of schism and heresy, and unbelief? When good and evil are traced to their true sources, verily in many cases the last will be first, and the first last !

I do not mean to imply that these simple considerations will remove all the trials of our smaller Parishes! the trial is a real one, and I think greater than ought to be allowed. I have already suggested that I think it would be well if our smaller livings were consolidated or held together in Plurality.

Meanwhile, my Brethren, whether in small Parishes or large, our real strength and comfort will be found in a closer companionship with God. Let me ask you, dear Brethren, to consider whether the recital of our daily office, as our Church directs, either openly or privately, would not give us ground for that true satisfaction, which comes with the consciousness of a daily duty done, and be a blessing both to ourselves and to our people. The daily office faithfully said, and the weekly Eucharist in small country Parishes, may hereafter be shown to have been the real power by which the great masses in our towns were converted. We know " the effectual fervent prayer of a righteous man availeth much."[6]   That we may not forget these our higher privileges and duties, I hope to hold, from time to time, in different centres of our Diocese, Special Days of Prayer and Instruction ; that we may be better able to understand the value of the souls entrusted to our care.   Through the great kindness of some well-known benefactors to this Diocese such days have been already held at Louth, and at Spalding, and at Alford : and please God, we shall be able to continue them.

If we can only bring our wills into more perfect union with God's Will, and learn to walk in His way, and abide His time, we shall not be discouraged.   We know that power belongeth unto God ; we know that the great head of the Church holds the seven stars in His right hand ; we know that He is actively present in the midst of the Churches ; we know that He knows our " works," " our labours," " our patience " ; and we know the condition upon which the reward will be given : " to him that overcometh."   It is intended therefore that we should have difficulties : difficulties should not discourage us, but remind us of the conditioned reward ; even the reward of sinless liberty, walking with Him in white ; the reward of resting with Him in eternal love and glory—" To him that " overcometh will I grant to sit with me in my Throne, " even as I also overcame and am set down with my " Father in His Throne"

[6] St. James, v. 16

To this great endless end it is the Will of our Heavenly Father that both we and our people should come, through the merits of Jesus Christ our Lord. Even so may it be for His sake.

Deo Gratias.

NOTE A.

Books are so easily laid aside and forgotten, that I shall not apologise for reminding you once more of the principles for understanding the Scriptures which Bishop Wordsworth has himself left us in his book on *Interpretation.*

In answer to the question, how are we to interpret the Bible, Bishop Wordsworth replies—First, by the right use of the two great faculties God has given us, Conscience and Reason, but these are not sufficient.

"Conscience is given us by God; it is His Voice within us. . . . . . but it is *not a Rule of Faith.*

"God has given us Reason, He also gives us Faith. Each of these has its proper office in Religion, and must be employed in its *proper place,* and in *that only.*"[1]

I. "First, our Reason is to be used in proving that Holy Scripture is the Word of God."

"Thus Reason leads us to the door of the Sanctuary. Faith will take us by the hand, and enable us to see the mysteries of the most Holy Place, and will speak to us of that blessed time, when we, who now watch by its light, shall pass into the true Holy of Holies in Heavenly places, and shall *see face to face, and know even as we are known.*"[2]

But Conscience and Reason are not enough. We need the supernatural aid of the Holy Spirit. "We cannot understand the Bible, except by the Light of the Holy Ghost, Who wrote the Bible." "He who would understand the Bible must love the Bible, he must revere the Bible, he must not treat it as a common book, he must regard it with holy awe, he must listen to it as God's oracle speaking from the Holy of Holies, he must pray over it, he must read it on his knees." "We must prepare ourselves for the study of the Bible by holiness of Life."

II. The Incarnate Word is the author and giver of the Written Word. He is also its true Interpreter.

1. *By His own word,* as in S. Luke xxiv. 45, "Then opened He their understanding, that they might understand the Scriptures"; and S. Luke xxiv. 27, "beginning at Moses and all the Prophets, He expounded unto them in all the Scriptures the things concerning Himself." "If you knock at the door of Scripture with the hand of Faith," says an ancient Father, "that door will be opened by Christ."

2. *By the ministry of His Apostles and Evangelists, e.g.,* S. Matt. ii. 15, "Out of Egypt have I called My Son"; 1 Cor. x. 4, "and that Rock was Christ."

3. *By the Bible itself, when we compare Spiritual things with Spiritual.* "Our Lord Jesus Christ, our great Prophet and Teacher, the incarnate Word of God, the Divine Interpreter of the Written Word, wills us to receive

---

(1) Cf. Dante, *Purgatorio,* c. xxvii., 126—142 :
—e se' venuto in parte
ov' io per me più oltre non discerno.

(2) Cf. Pascal, opuscules, Preface sur le Traité du Vide, ed. Ch. Louandre, p. 583.
"In Theology it is Authority which has the principal weight. . . . . The case is very different with things which are in the domain of the Senses and of Human Reason. . . . . . Authority is useless then . . . . This essential difference between Theology and Physical Science may well inspire us with sorrow for the blindness of some who apply Authority alone to Natural Philosophy, instead of resorting to Reason and Experiment. And it may also fill us with horror for the wickedness of others, who employ Reason alone in Theology, instead of appealing to the Authority of Holy Scripture and the Fathers of the Church. Our duty is to excite the courage of those timid spirits, who dare not find out anything in Physics, and confound the insolence of those rash adventurers who broach novelties in Theology."

Scripture as one luminous whole. If we wish to understand the Bible, we must not separate one portion of it from another; we must endeavour to ascertain its sense by comparing spiritual things with spiritual. He does it in order to teach us that all parts of Scripture are dependent on one another, like joints in a well organized body, or like parts of a beautiful building; He does it in order that we may not confine our attention to *any one part* of Scripture, to the neglect of others, but may carefully consider the whole."
"We confess that the living waters of His grace flow freely to all. We hear the Holy Spirit's voice, *to every one that thirsteth, come ye to the waters, and he that hath no money, come ye, buy and eat. I will give unto him that is athirst, of the fountain of the water of life freely.*

"But, brethren, we should not rightly interpret the mind of the Holy Ghost, if we did not combine such gracious intimations as these with His own Divine declaration in other parts of that Word, that the Living Waters of His Grace flow freely indeed to all, but also flow regularly in certain rivers and channels, especially in the Holy Scriptures, and in the Holy Sacraments, and in Prayer, and in Confirmation."

"Almighty God has not revealed all truth in one book of Holy Scripture; but He has made one portion of Scripture ministerial and subsidiary to another. He has made the Book of Genesis to reflect light on the Book of Revelation, and He has made the Book of Revelation to illustrate the Book of Genesis."

4. *By the Universal Church.*—Christ is the Everlasting Word; He is the author of the written Word; He is the interpreter of the Bible. He has given us the Scriptures by the Holy Spirit, and he expounds the Scriptures by the same Spirit, and that Spirit is in His Universal Church. He declares to us the true meaning of Holy Scripture, in all necessary points of Christian doctrine, in her Creeds and Confessions of Faith." "Christ first declares His universal supremacy, '*All power is given unto Me in heaven and earth.*' And what follows? A commission, extending to all place and time, '*Go ye and teach all nations. . . .* Here is the root of the Christian Faith. It is more ancient than the New Testament."

"In the Ancient Creeds of the Church Universal, Jesus Christ, who has promised to be present with His Church, speaks to us by His Spirit, and declares to us the true sense of the Bible."

"Let it not be alleged, that we thus elevate the Church, to the disparagement of Christ her Lord. No, we contend for Christ's universal supremacy; we proclaim His perpetual presence, and continued operation in the Church . . . Christ is the Head, and the Church is His Body; and He animates the Body. Let us not separate the Head from the Body; let us not divide Christ from the Church. Unless we have *both* we cannot have *either*—"Let us therefore have both; let us cleave to the Body for the sake of the Head; let us hold fast to the Church for the sake of Christ." But by separating the Church from the Bible they forfeit the blessings of both. Let us, brethren, endeavour, by God's help, to maintain both—the Bible is God's Word, the Church is God's House, let us reverently listen to that Word, preached and interpreted by His Spirit abiding in His House."

I cannot help adding the following words from a Paper read at the Wakefield Church Congress, 1886, on the *Devotional Study of the Psalter :*—

"The vast and varied literature to which we give the name of the "Bible," enters upon every field of intellectual enquiry; it touches upon every topic that is of interest to man. The unrolling of that literature, the order and course of revelation, the philosophy and the science, the poetry and the history, the date and authorship of the various books, the text and the interpretation of the text, all fall under the province of the student. He will follow the

---

methods which are proper to each subject of enquiry. Devotion, by her loyalty to the Holy Spirit, is bound to accept the conclusions which study reaches, however cherished may be the traditions which those conclusions overthrow."

"It is the function of "devotion" to give life; it is the office of "study" to shed light. A devotional use of the Bible apart from critical, systematic study is dangerous. It is sure to place self where the Church ought to be placed, it separates the Bible from the Church, and both from history, and falls into schism or heresy."

NOTE B.

It may seem superfluous to mention any Books on the Church, yet I venture to hope it may not be quite so, at least to all, especially if the point of view is remembered which has been pressed above namely : that many of us have neglected a full consideration of the clause in the Creed which expresses our belief in the Church, and that we too often avoid the full weight of the evidence, from the sacrifice which it would involve in our social or ministerial position. The divisions of Christendom have made some of us almost despair of Unity, and thus we have been tempted to lose faith in the Church.

What is required is that we should diligently and prayerfully consider a sufficiency of the old evidences, and be prepared to follow God, wheresoever He may lead us, and to give up all for the Kingdom of Heaven's sake. Perhaps in this way there may be found opportunities for self-sacrifice even now in England, not less in their way than in the great work abroad.

The Pastoral Epistles, with the Modern Commentaries : and of the ancient, S. Chrysostom's Homilies.

The Apostolic Fathers. Lightfoot. Holland.

S. Irenæus Adversus Hæreses.

Tertullian de Præscriptione.

S. Cyprian de Unitate, and many of his Epistles.

S. Augustine de Unitate, and all the Treatises Contra Donatistas. They set forth the evil of Schism, and show the principles on which Controversy should be settled, viz., Scripture and the Appeal to the Church throughout the world and a General Council.

S. Vincent of Lerins, The Commonitorium. Ed. C. Marriott, 1851.

Hooker, Eccl. Pol., Bk. vii. Jer. Taylor, Episcopacy Vindicated. Bp. Bilson, Perpetual Government of the Church of Christ.

These give sufficient summaries of the Historical Evidence.

I should like to remind you yet again of Theophilus Anglicanus, and the cheap abridgment, Elements of Instruction on the Church, by Ch. Wordsworth, D.D., Bishop of Lincoln, 1879. This might easily be adapted for Parochial Lectures.

Notes on the Four General Councils, by W. Bright, D.D., Professor of Eccl. History in the University of Oxford.

Lectures on the Holy Catholic Church, Canon Ashwell, 1878.

Dr. Liddon's Sermon, "A Father in Christ," ed. 3d.

Dr. Moberley, "The Great Forty Days."

Of Special Treatises on the Work and Character of the Clergy, showing what manner of men we ought to be, we might mention :

The Old Patristic Treatises—

S. Gregory Nazianzen Apologeticus printed in C. Marriott's Anelecta Christiana.

S. Ambrose de Officiis Ministrorum.

S. Chrysostom de Sacerdotio.

S. Jerome, Ep. ad Nepotianum.

S. Gregory de Cura Pastorali, ed. with Translation by Rev. H. R. Bramley.

Of English Writers, among many we may mention—

George Herbert's Country Parson.

Bishop Burnet's Pastoral Care.

Bishop Bull's Sermon on the great Difficulties and Dangers of the Priestly Office.

Blunt's (Prof. J. J.) Parish Priest.

Bishop Wilberforce's Ordination Addresses.

Bishop Woodford, "The Great Commission."

Heygate, W. E., Ember Hours.

The Priest in His Inner Life.   Masters.

NOTE C.

1.—We may consider the Standard of our present Rubrics.

(*a*) For our people the rule is that every Parishioner should communicate at least three times in the year, of which Easter is to be one.

(*b*) For our Clergy, where there are many living together, all are to communicate every Sunday at the least. This points to a weekly Communion at least as a standard for the Clergy.

(*c*) The Rubric which begins "Upon the Sundays and other Holy Days (if there be no Communion,)" suggests Communion on Sundays and Saint Days as the rule ; as of course does the provision of a special Collect, Epistle, and Gospel.

(*d*) The Rubrics for the use of the Proper Prefaces for Christmas, Easter, Ascension Day, and Whitsunday, emphasize daily Communion during the octaves.

(*e*) The Rubric for small Parishes contemplates a Communion, provided *three* are ready to communicate with the Priest. Assuming for the moment that such persons might communicate monthly a band of *twelve* or *fifteen* persons would secure a weekly Celebration.

2.—The Standard apparently attainable at present.

(*a*) We have no discipline to enforce the rule of Communion *three* times a year on all our Parishioners.

(*b*) It would seem from the returns for the Diocese that to have one-tenth of the population on the communicants' roll is a standard that might be attained in average Parishes. In the large Town Parishes this standard is rarely reached, while in our small Country Parishes the proportion is sometimes one-fifth or one-third.

James Williamson, Printer, High Street, Lincoln.

Lightning Source UK Ltd.
Milton Keynes UK
UKOW02f0127221013

219514UK00012B/1264/P